D0982703

Long-Life Learning is a lifeboat for those of us swimming in the sea of confusing—and often contradicting—narratives about the future of learning, working, and living. Throughout, Michelle brings thoughtful and diverse evidence to bear on a host of pressing challenges facing not just schools but all of society and offers a deeply integrative set of insights from her years as a student of disruptive innovation to chart a better way forward—robots and all.

— Brian Fleming, Vice President of Innovation and Strategy, Southern New Hampshire University

Without handwringing about the rise of automation, or finger-pointing at our current systems of education and employment, *Long-Life Learning* advances a vision of the future that puts the needs of workers at the center. Recasting us all as "working learners," Michelle Weise illustrates not just the value of repeated returns to learning, but the critical importance of seamlessly interweaving education and work throughout our careers.

—Van Ton-Quinlivan, CEO, Futuro Health

In *Long-Life Learning*, Michelle Weise articulates the critical need for adults to access an ever-evolving menu of learning and workforce skills development to remain relevant in the future economy and a 100-year work life.

— Deborah Quazzo, Managing Partner, GSV Ventures

LONG
LIFE
LEARNING

MICHELLE R. WEISE

STRADA EDUCATION NETWORK, INC.

LONG
LIFE
LEARNING

PREPARING FOR JOBS
THAT DON'T EVEN
EXIST YET

WILEY

Published by John Wiley & Sons, Inc., Hoboken, New Jersey.
Published simultaneously in Canada.

For general information on our other products and services or for technical support, please contact our Customer Care Department within the United States at (800) 762-2974, outside the United States at (317) 572-3993 or fax (317) 572-4002.

Wiley publishes in a variety of print and electronic formats and by print-on-demand. Some material included with standard print versions of this book may not be included in e-books or in print-on-demand. If this book refers to media such as a CD or DVD that is not included in the version you purchased, you may download this material at http:// booksupport.wiley.com. For more information about Wiley products, visit www.wiley.com.

Library of Congress Cataloging-in-Publication Data:

Names: Weise, Michelle R., author.
Title: Long life learning : preparing for jobs that don't even exist yet / Michelle R. Weise.
Description: Hoboken, New Jersey : John Wiley & Sons, Inc., 2021. | Includes index.
Identifiers: LCCN 2020030474 (print) | LCCN 2020030475 (ebook) | ISBN 9781119597483 (cloth) | ISBN 9781119597513 (adobe pdf) | ISBN 9781119597520 (epub)
Subjects: LCSH: Employees—Training of. | Career education. | Occupational training. | Vocational education. | Manpower planning.
Classification: LCC HF5549.5.T7 W3879 2021 (print) | LCC HF5549.5.T7 (ebook) | DDC 650.1/3—dc23
LC record available at https://lccn.loc.gov/2020030474
LC ebook record available at https://lccn.loc.gov/2020030475

Cover image: © Maria_Galybina/Getty Images
Cover design: Wiley

Printed in the United States of America

SKY10021600_101220

For Mike, Noe, and Logan, the loves of my life,
and for the risk takers, innovators, and coalition builders,
this book is for you.

CONTENTS

INTRODUCTION: AN ABIDING
HOPE FOR THE FUTURE

One of the great privileges of my life was working with Clayton
Christensen, the godfather of the theories of disruptive innovation. I coauthored a few pieces with him, including a short book on
disruption in postsecondary education.[1]

After his much-too-early death in January 2020, I've reflected
a great deal on how his theories have given me the foundation for
a more hopeful stance toward the future. This, to me, is the most
profound takeaway of disruption. It is not, as so many assume, the
key to doomsday predictions about an industry. Instead, the theories
of disruption are powerful because they provide a constructive and
positive lens through which to analyze the unknown and the nascent.

Clay's theories give us pause as soon as we start to dismiss something that smacks of low quality, because it is precisely at that moment
that we should wonder if there's something we should be paying attention to—something that might be just "good enough" (his words) to
gain traction with people whose alternative is nothing at all.[2] He called
this population *nonconsumers*.

Prior to the pandemic, my team of education and workforce
researchers at Strada Education Network's Institute for the Future
of Work was focused on these nonconsumers, the people being left
behind by the great deficiencies of our American education and
workforce infrastructure. Over the course of more than 100 hour-long

interviews, we listened to working-age adults displaced by the 2008 financial crisis who were unable to recover while the top 1 percent of the American labor market captured 85 percent of the income growth in the years following the recession.[3] Throughout this book, you will hear from many of these displaced workers.

They include a high school graduate who was promised opportunities for growth at her local pharmacy but never saw those promotions come to pass due to the constant churn in staff and managers. They are also the people whose caregiving responsibilities—for young children, aging parents, or family members with disabilities—make it impossible to fit into the one-size-fits-all structure of many educational institutions.

Their personal experiences reveal how ill-suited our current postsecondary education and workforce systems are at facilitating seamless, flexible, and cost-effective learning pathways for people to keep up with the emerging demands of the economy. If students don't follow the typical two- or four-year college experience, our systems do not make it easy for them to return and retrain in the future. Learners are left to force-fit nonlinear realities into a rigidly linear system.

Capturing these small, poignant stories has been vital for my research and for understanding the obstacles new consumers of education face. It's also something that I've rarely encountered in other scholars' research on the future of work. Most of the analyses and research get bogged down in the *what* as opposed to the *who*. Researchers have been obsessed with quantifying and understanding the changing nature of work by anticipating mass unemployment, long periods of painful adjustment, and the enduring consequences of new technological advancements. Anxiety about the future of work can quickly devolve into a kind of fearmongering. It seems that almost every day there's a paralyzing new fact or figure about the future of work.

The truth is, we don't have to pinpoint the actual number or the specific jobs or tasks we can expect to see automated in the years to come. At a certain point, the statistics become overwhelming. As I write this introduction, COVID-19 has paralyzed the world economy, and the number of unemployment claims in the United States alone has topped 45 million—an unfathomable number.[4] The problem is almost too big and amorphous to grapple with through statistics alone. Numbers don't account for the human cost of the problem—the real lives at the center—and the impact on you and me.

Author Daniel Pink describes the virus as the "great unmasking of problems that were in plain sight . . . there were always these fundamental cracks in the system."[5] Indeed, even before the pandemic, more than 41 million working-age Americans were seeking more direct connections to good jobs and good wages, but they kept falling through the cracks because of the limited way in which we train and hire our workforce.[6]

The global pandemic has laid bare how fragile our multiple, fragmented systems of K–12 education, postsecondary education, and workforce training are. For quite some time, these siloed and unintegrated systems have neglected millions of people looking to access the relevant information, funding, advising, support, and skills training they need in order to advance.

Adults have never had easy access to on- and off-ramps in and out of learning and work. Our systems are brittle and were never designed for continuous returns to learning. Sure, bits and pieces and discrete solutions exist, but they are neither connected nor integrated, especially for the people who need the most help in finding a way forward.

Newly laid-off workers don't have the technologies and tools they need to analyze their talents, bring them to the surface, and assess their skill gaps. They want information about how to choose the right career pathways—the type real-time labor market information and consumer reviews provide. They want guidance on which pathways will be most effective, targeted, and affordable in helping them grow and thrive in the labor market. But there are no human guides or support services to coach them.

Part I of my book touches on all of the barriers—structural, cultural, and political—that have stymied the advancement of millions of workers and learners. The first three chapters delve into the obstacles that make progress feel impossible for adults today.

From this complexity, we move to a more positive vision of the future. Part II introduces the constructive mental model of a new learning ecosystem that will show us the way, help us learn, endorse that learning, help us pay, and get us hired. Each chapter in this section delves deeply into each of these five guiding principles: A new learning ecosystem must be **navigable**, **supportive**, **targeted**, **integrated**, and **transparent**.

To illuminate each aspect of a lifelong learning ecosystem, we begin with what we're hearing from the new consumers of education, then move into the predicaments and barriers that hold their problems in place, and conclude by providing solutions and revealing the seeds of innovation that are helping more people launch into better opportunities. The solutions featured are not comprehensive lists but instead are meant to be illustrative of the kinds of building blocks we need to see more of in a better-functioning learning ecosystem.

We have to move from the future we don't want to the future we *do* want. We must practice thinking bigger and more boldly about the future we wish to create. In this book, we identify what's working now and consider how to replicate those advances for more working learners.

It takes significant energy and deliberate practice to think expansively and optimistically about what we can do now to prepare for an uncertain world of work. If we invest today in the infrastructure of the learning ecosystem of that future, we will ensure that generations of learners will be equipped with the relevant skills to thrive in the jobs of tomorrow. The *doing* will not come easily, but the opportunity is clear for us to stitch together new and existing programs and solutions that can serve as engines of upward mobility for millions of Americans, including you and me.

Part I
From a Rigged System

1 A 100-Year Work Life

People's life plans used to be a bit more straightforward. We were supposed to pack in some education early on in our lives, with the expectation that we would work and build a career—maybe even raise a family—and then retire. *Learn, earn, rest.*

Futurists and experts on aging and longevity are now suggesting that we can expect to live longer and that human life spans will extend decades longer than we had anticipated. The authors of *The 100-Year Life* explain: "For most of the last two hundred years there has been a steady increase in life expectancy. More precisely, the best data currently available suggests that since 1840 there has been an increase in life expectancy of three months for every year. That's two to three years of life added for every decade. . . . And perhaps more importantly, there is no sign that the trend is levelling off."[1]

With advances in health care, medicine, and disease control as well as improvements in general living conditions, we have "found a way to slow down the process of bodily decay that was given to us by nature," writes aging specialist Johannes Koettl, "a truly remarkable development that no other species has achieved before."[2] The Global AgeWatch Index Report anticipates that by 2100, the number of people aged 80 and over will increase more than sevenfold, from 125 million to 944 million.[3] Some are even suggesting that the first people to live to be 150 years old have already been born.[4]

Let's think about that for a moment: 150 years.

The simple extension of our life span suddenly forces us to consider the dramatic lengthening of our work lives. Will the careers of the future last 60, 80, or 100 years?

This is a very different kind of future of work.

More Than 12 Jobs in a Lifetime

Already, workers who are 55 and older are staying in the workforce at historically high rates, well into their late 60s and even 70s.[5] And job transitions have become an established part of life. In the United States alone, 10,000 baby boomers will turn 65 every day from now until 2030,[6] and many of them will have experienced at least 12 job changes by the time they retire.[7]

With this new time horizon, it becomes hard to imagine a straight line from education to work and, finally, retirement. Gone are the days of retiring at age 65 and living on a guaranteed pension from one or a few employers that defined a person's career. Rather, the number of job transitions will only increase with time, as people confront longer and more turbulent work lives.

The notion of a 100-year work life is arresting and quickly snaps our education system into sharp relief by upending so many of our working assumptions. Our default mental model has been that education is largely a one-and-done experience situated on the front end of our development through young adulthood. This perception is further reinforced by societal expectations and financial policies that suggest that higher education is for young adults.[8]

Cast in this new light, however, two, four, or six years of college front-loaded at the beginning of a 100-year work life suddenly seem deeply inadequate. Technology's transformation of nearly every facet of our economy means that we will all need to develop new skills and knowledge at a pace—and on a scale—never before seen.

Advancements will continue to give rise to entirely new kinds of jobs and careers, ones that we cannot even begin to name.

It's already been happening. In 2014, LinkedIn's top jobs were ones that hadn't existed five years earlier—roles like iOS/Android developer, UI/UX designer, cloud manager, big data architect, and social media intern.[9] How many more as-yet unknown jobs will we hold in a 100-year work life?

The Future of Work = The Future of Learning

We are all going to have to prepare for jobs that don't even exist yet. Enter the concept of long-life learning. Through the lens of human longevity, the future of work becomes inextricably tied to the future of learning. In a 100-year work life, we may find ourselves in a state of continuous pivots—20 to 30 job transitions might become the new normal. Ongoing skill development will become a way of life.

No matter our current station, we will all become working learners, always flexing between working and learning, or juggling both at the same time—looping continuously in and out of learning and work and navigating more job transitions than we ever dreamed possible.

Moreover, we see how we are not artificially separated from the future of learning and work, as if it was some sort of alternate reality—for other people, not me, at least not now. This is not a future from which we are somehow removed. The concept of long-life learning makes our mandate so much clearer: Education and training will be more important than ever, because those future workers are all of *us*.

Where Are the On- and Off-Ramps?

The challenge is that we can't access many on- or off-ramps in and out of learning and work today. Educators, policymakers, and funders give a lot of lip service to the concept of lifelong learning, but this talk rarely translates into action. In fact, resources and funding are often geared toward the traditional 18- to 24-year-old college-going population and less often to working adults, the growing majority of learners. There is little investment in the systems, architecture, and infrastructure needed to facilitate seamless movements in and out of learning and work.

The current system of higher education is not forgiving. Today, close to 70 percent of high school graduates go on to college, but they do not always complete their degrees.[10] Instead, they "stop out." They take the one and only off-ramp available, are subsequently labeled "college dropouts," and are then often punished further with some student loan debt.[11] In total, 36 million people in the United States made it into college; they just didn't make it through or out of college.[12]

For most adults, taking time off work to attend classes at a local, brick-and-mortar community college or four-year institution will not be the answer. A one-, two-, or four-year college program may be a bridge too far in terms of both the time to credential and the full cost of attendance, including the lost wages associated with attending school instead of working more hours.

We must therefore begin prototyping more flexible reskilling and upskilling pathways for the future. We will have to change our approach and put some teeth into the concept of lifelong learning, an idea that has been good in theory (decades old!) but slow to catch fire. We agree with the concept but have not been moved to change our behavior and invest in the much-needed infrastructure for continuous development and advancement.

But once we understand that that *we* are the ones who will be affected—that the future of workers is about us—the fourth wall, or the imaginary wall between those people and us, breaks down. We will all have to harness the power of education over and over again through-out a longer work life. And we will need more on-demand pathways that tie education to economic relevance—more seamless ways to loop in and out of learning and work. *Learn, earn, learn, earn, learn, earn.*

Are We Future-Proof?

As periodic returns to learning become the new normal, which skills will we need to develop? Kevin Kelly, forecasting future tech trends in his book *The Inevitable*, puts it this way: "This is not a race against the machines. If we race against them, we lose. This is a race *with* the machines. You'll be paid in the future based on how well you work with robots. Ninety percent of your coworkers will be unseen machines. Most of what you do will not be possible without them. And there will be a blurry line between what you do and what they do."[13]

There will be certain activities that humans will have to relinquish to computers. Economist David Autor suggests that the more clearly we can describe a task, the easier it may be to create rules for it; mathematics, logical deduction, and encoding quantitative relationships—really any work that involves "a set of formal logical tools"—can be automated.[14] The harder the skill is to describe or enunciate, however, the more resistant it may be to computerization.

Autor named this phenomenon Polanyi's paradox after the Hungarian economist, philosopher, and chemist Michael Polanyi, who famously explains in his work *The Tacit Dimension* that "we know more than we can tell."[15] Polanyi explains that our tacit knowledge is greater than our ability to explicitly describe how we engage with the world around us.

Think about describing how you ride a bike or a horse, how you crack an egg on the side of a bowl, how you adjust your grasp when a cup of coffee is slipping out of your hands, or how you persuade someone when writing an essay. There are skills and rules in our human knowledge and capability that lie beneath consciousness. Polanyi's paradox helps us understand how we can thrive in the work of the future.

Automation Makes Us More Human

What is core to the human experience, or that which we do effortlessly as humans, may empower us to outcompete machines and coordinate better with them. A large part of the literature on the work of the future underscores a growing need for *human skills*, or capabilities that robots or machine learning cannot simulate. The McKinsey Global Institute notes that "as machines take on ever more of the predictable activities of the workday, these skills will be at a premium. Automation could make us all more human."[16]

Human skills and abilities go by many names: soft, social-emotional, noncognitive, power, foundational, common, transferable, baseline, 21st century, employability, workforce readiness, interpersonal, talent, life, and professional skills. More and more research is pointing to these human skills as a way of categorizing our human strengths and defining our competitive edge over robots and machines.[17] And there is a tremendous amount of emphasis on attributes such as high emotional or social intelligence, adaptability, flexibility, judgment, resilience, systems thinking, and communication.[18] Indeed, we can easily imagine how machines might fail to understand nonverbal gestures and cues in order to guess at or sense the emotional state of a person. Machines are not as good as we are at reading distress, fear, worry, confusion, elation, or tone.

Not only will these skills become more important with time, but real-time labor market information also confirms that employers are already in desperate search of these human skills. An Emsi analysis of more than 36 million job postings, resumes, and social profiles shows that in just the first half of 2018, the skills in highest demand were leadership, management, communications, sales, and problem solving.[19] (See Figure 1.1.)

This all sounds promising: Human skills are in higher demand than ever, and we appear to be well positioned (as humans) to demonstrate those uniquely human skills.

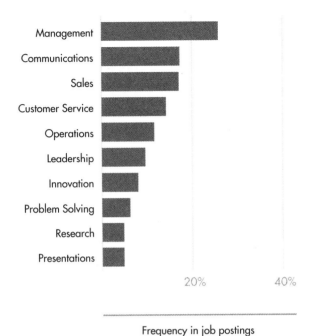

Frequency in job postings

Figure 1.1 Human skills like communication, leadership, and problem solving are among the most common skills employers list in job postings.

Source: Robot-Ready: Human+ Skills for the Future of Work. Emsi job posting analytics, 2018. © 2018, Strada Education Network.

When Humans Fall Down on the Job of Being Human

But just because we're human doesn't necessarily mean we're great at the human side of work. In fact, human skills require practice; they are not innate. In his book *Humans Are Underrated*, author Geoff Colvin asserts, "At just the time when skills of human interaction are becoming the key to people's economic value, young people are abandoning those very skills in favor of digital communication .... Empathy has become a wasting muscle."[20] The work of the future increasingly demands more social and emotional intelligence, but the opportunities for us to broaden our human skills and define our competitive advantage have been progressively diminishing in our day-to-day lives.

First off, we're looking at each other less and spending more time on screens. Colvin discusses the various ways in which we as humans perceive differences in the slightest changes in facial expressions. He describes the work of the psychologist Paul Ekman, who has researched the 40 muscles in the human face, which can combine into over 10,000 expressions—3,000 of which have something to do with emotion.[21] The effect of more hours spent on screens means that we are spending less time practicing our human skills in person with others, decoding facial expressions, body language, nonverbal cues, and tone. As a result, advancing technology is "doing much more than changing the nature of work," Colvin argues. "It's also changing us."[22]

What's in Your Bubble?

We are also relating less and less with people with whom we differ. The algorithms that undergird most of our apps have turned our social relationships into bubbles. Back in 2014, Eli Pariser gave a stirring TED talk called "Beware Online 'Filter Bubbles'" in which he talked about the "invisible, algorithmic editing" that turns our World Wide Web into "a web of one."[23]

There is no such thing as a standard Google search result, Pariser explained. Each of our search results looks different even if we use the same exact keyword. Pariser said, "[T]he Internet is showing us what it thinks we want to see, but not necessarily what we need to see. . . . And what's in your filter bubble depends on who you are, and it depends on what you do. But the thing is that you don't decide what gets in. And more importantly, you don't actually see what gets edited out." These bubbles mean that we no longer have access to "a balanced information diet."

How we relate to one another and reconcile differing views is diminishing drastically because of new forms of artificial intelligence (AI). We're surrounded by things with which we agree as opposed to issues or viewpoints that might challenge our thinking or make us feel uncomfortable. It takes practice to see things from another person's point of view, but it's impossible to empathize if we're never exposed to those ideas in the first place.

Hybrid Skills: Human + Technical Skills

All learners will need to develop, practice, and strengthen these durable and more human skills over the course of a lifetime. However, human skills alone are not enough. The jobs of the future will be hybrid in nature. Human resources expert Josh Bersin explains that these new hybrid jobs "do not lend themselves to static job descriptions and simple job titles. They are jobs that require technical, industry, managerial, and integrated thinking skills; they often require skills in communication, persuasion, and teamwork."[24]

The skills needed for these jobs will also be hybrid. Employers demand intellectual dexterity and technical expertise in equal measure, or human + technical skills: emotional intelligence + artificial intelligence; ethics + logic; or communication + programming.[25] It's not the "Tyranny of the OR," as author Jim Collins describes it, but rather the "Genius of the AND."[26] The most valuable workers now and in the future will be those who can combine human + technical skills (human+ for short), and adapt to the changing needs of the workplace.

Deep learning AI, as author Scott Hartley puts succinctly in *The Fuzzy and the Techie*, requires "deep-thinking humans."[27] Problems can scale out of control via tech-enabled environments. Writer Lee Rainie explains, "Connected things and connected people become more useful, more powerful, but also more hair-trigger and more destructive because their power is multiplied by a networking effect. The more connections they have, the more capacity they have for good and harmful purposes."[28] Oddly, it is Facebook's own COO, Sheryl Sandberg, whose platform has been implicated in some of these global disasters, who said it so well: "When you write a line of code, you can affect a lot of people."[29]

When a company like one of the Big Five tech giants experiments, the implications are vast. Each decision on each product has "volume-impact repercussions," explains Gregory Chan, an engineering project manager at Apple.[30] There are no precedents for dealing with the issues that tech companies will encounter when developing a new product that millions of people around the world will immediately adopt—sometimes in a matter of hours. In an interview, Chan reflected on his general education requirements for college and expressed his relief in having taken an ethics class alongside his mechanical engineering courses. A stronger grasp of human+ skills has enabled him to consider the voluminous repercussions of the choices that get made.

Enough Technical Skills to Be Dangerous

To be robot-ready, we're not only going to have to practice our human skills, but we're also going to need some domain knowledge to assess the work of the machines. All of us will need to have enough technical skills to be dangerous and intervene at the right times. The balance is critical.

Finland may therefore have the right approach with its "1 percent" AI initiative. With the support of government and private companies, the country is trying to teach 1 percent of its population (approximately 55,000 people) the basic concepts that lie at the root of machine learning.[31]

AI is complicated and abstract. The decisions and outputs of machine learning technologies are not always explainable, and that lack of transparency and explanation won't be acceptable as AI penetrates more parts of our lives, especially the medical and legal fields and other areas where human lives are at stake. People must ask: What kinds of ethical choices are happening on the back end of programming that need to be more explicit? Are these technologies leveraging biased computational formulas and unfairly discriminating against people because they have been trained on flawed data?

In its current format, AI is deeply problematic because it is being deployed widely across all sectors, but very few companies—fewer than a third, according to the authors of *Human + Machine*—"have a high degree of confidence in the fairness and auditability of their AI systems, and less than half have similar confidence in the safety of those systems."[32] What does it say that we've already become so reliant on these technologies, and yet we don't fully trust the algorithms that undergird them?

Human+ skills are critical. Working learners must understand what AI is, so that they can control what Andrew Ng, founder of the Google Brain Deep Learning Project, calls "the new electricity."[33] Just like electricity, AI will impact everything. Therefore, technical skills will be just as critical as the human values, morals, and principles needed to pair with them.

Otherwise, problems may scale. Theoretical physicist Stephen Hawking captured our societal dilemma well when he said that "success in creating effective AI could be the biggest event in the history of our civilization. Or the worst."

America should be taking note of Finland's initiative. Empowering people with the basic principles of AI, along with its potential pitfalls, is a strategic first step in equipping citizens for future civic engagement while also preparing them for the world ahead.

Visualizing Long-Life Learning

In many ways, human+ skills are similar to the concept of the
T-shaped learner, which entered the lexicon in the 1990s. The T-shape
describes the combination of an individual's breadth of knowledge
with the depth of their technical expertise. (See Figure 1.2.)

But, in a world in which our work lives become longer and more
unpredictable, even the concept of a T-shaped person will become out-
moded. This figure will change shape and turn jagged as an individual
moves through life, acquiring new skills along the way. Sometimes this
will involve a broadening of knowledge; at other times, more verticality
or additional technical skills will be called for, depending on our context. (See Figure 1.3.)

In a 100-year work life, there will no longer be a single transition
from schooling to work. As we try to make sense of a longer, more

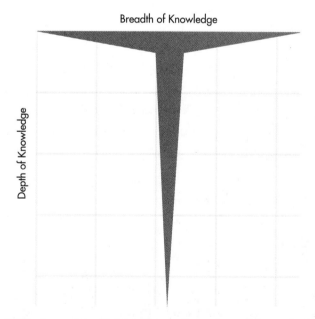

**Figure 1.2 T-shaped individuals combine broad knowledge and
skills with deep expertise in a narrow field.**

turbulent work life, we must anticipate that learning and continual skill development will become a way of life.

At the same time, this won't necessarily be a linear process. Stanford University's d.school (design school) came up with the concept of an open loop university, where, over a six-year period, learners could begin at any time in their lives and loop in and out of the school to gain skills, access community and expertise, and loop back out to apply that new knowledge.[34] The challenge, of course, is that even six years will not suffice, as working learners will have to loop in and out of cycles of earning and learning over a dramatically longer period of time.

There will need to be more on- and off-ramps for long-life learning. Picture a cloverleaf interchange off a highway. We'll need to harness the power of education just as if we were taking that cloverleaf, gaining what we need, and smoothly reentering the workforce highway in a seamless fashion.

Of course, this begs the question: Where exactly will we be going to access long-life learning? Where will we develop our human+ skills?

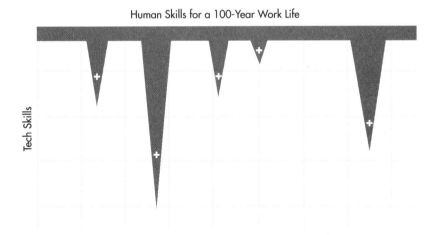

Figure 1.3 Returning to learning throughout a 100-year work life.

The Never-Ending Debate on Education versus Workforce Training

Learning and work are becoming inseparable . . . indeed one could argue that this is precisely what it means to have a knowledge economy or a learning society. It follows that if work is becoming learning, then learning needs to become work—and universities need to become alive to the possibilities.

—Michael Barber, Katelyn Donnelly, and Saad Rizvi[35]

While future-of-work researchers are discussing the skills needed for the 20 or 30 job transitions to come, higher education appears to be stuck, perseverating on just that first transition from young adulthood to the workforce. The long-standing debate revolves around whether institutions of higher education bear any responsibility for the preparedness of graduates for the workforce. Reluctant to train learners for work, colleges and universities remain wary of aligning their programs and majors to the needs of today's rapidly evolving labor market, fearing that college might resemble too closely vocational or career technical training programs.

Academics have historically separated teaching and scholarship as an enterprise distinct from vocational training. Utility was what trade, graduate, and professional schools were for, whereas college was the space and time for students to pursue their passions and gain a global perspective. Regular opinion pieces and articles in the journals *Inside Higher Ed* and *The Chronicle of Higher Education* reveal this strong sentiment.

In one example, Tim Johnston from the Council of Colleges of Arts and Sciences explains that there is a "'mistaken emphasis' on a student's first job out of college. 'A college education really is a preparation for life, it's not training for the first job you get,' he said, adding that most people these days have 'changeable and unpredictable' career paths."[36] In a different piece for the New England Board of

Higher Education, George McCully argues that "education certainly includes training, but is both broader and deeper, intensely personal and social—focusing on the cultivation of values. Education is more about *who*, training is more about *what*, students are and will become in their subsequent lives and careers."[37]

Training for work implies a narrower kind of learning experience. Critics sustain this argument in order to suggest that employers should therefore own and leverage workforce training to keep workers up to speed on "useful knowledge and skills" for a rapidly evolving labor market.[38] College is much better suited, McCully argues, for the "permanent and characteristic mission of higher education," or things that do not go "in and out of fashion with changes in economies or technologies." This is an argument about the timelessness of a college education—learning that is not specifically tailored toward work or "the *what*," as McCully calls it.

This never-ending debate highlights a puzzling disconnect: Educators uphold the notion of durable learning that can last a lifetime and nod vigorously whenever the concept of lifelong learning comes up. But lifelong learning does not occur in some sort of vacuum, untethered to the world of work. Nor is it just about an older worker pursuing his or her curiosity or passion. Learning for a lifetime is also motivated by the practical and utilitarian needs of workers seeking to survive and thrive in their work lives. These discussions cannot be separated, as if something unique happens in a college education, detached from the learning and experience gained through work.

A False Choice

It makes little sense to continue to pit a college education against workforce training. The American Academy of Arts and Sciences put it best in its report on the future of undergraduate education: "Today, the long-standing debate over the value of a liberal arts education versus a more applied postsecondary program presents a false choice."[39]

Education and work are one and the same. As economist Anthony
P. Carnevale writes: "The inescapable reality is that ours is a society
based on work. Increasing the economic relevance of education should,
if done properly, extend the ability of educators to empower Americans to work in the world, rather than retreat from it."[40] Carnevale
describes it as a modern wage equation:

> If you write an equation for earnings, one of the first variables you
> put in it to predict earnings is your education, your field of study,
> but then the variables that start having real power are what you
> learn on the job, your opportunity to learn on the job—formally,
> informally—and the power of the technology that you work
> with . . . And remember, you may go to college for one year, two
> years, three years, four years, five, but you're going to work for 40,
> 45, or 50 years. So, it's naturally the case that the most powerful
> teacher is the job itself.[41]

Through the lens of human longevity, work becomes inextricably
tied to education. This isn't and shouldn't be a philosophical debate.
The artificial separation between career readiness skills and generalist or
humanist skills exists only at an academic level. In the lived experiences
of learners, work is a major motivating factor. For over 50 years, The
Freshman Survey has asked first-time full-time students why they go to
college. "[T]o be able to get a job" has always been the number 1 or 2
reason—certainly the top reason since the recession.[42]

Beyond freshmen learners, the same motivation holds true for
adults age 18 to 64 in the United States. Between 2017 and 2019,
Strada partnered with Gallup to survey over 350,000 residents about
their educational experiences. The clear message from learners is
that they enroll in higher education for job and work outcomes—54
percent of the respondents said that job and career outcomes were
their primary motivation, compared to 22 percent for the next more
general reason of learning more and gaining knowledge.[43] In another
nationally representative survey in late April 2020, during the first

surge of the COVID-19 pandemic, that number bumped up to 68 percent of Americans looking to enroll in the next six months in order to reskill and upskill.[44]

The rhetoric around education versus training elides the career trajectories of people today who are bearing the brunt of a misalignment between their education and the jobs they are able to attain. In that same Strada-Gallup consumer insights work, few college graduates from almost any of the disciplines (except health care and education) actually found their coursework relevant or helpful. STEM majors were almost as dissatisfied as language and philosophy majors with only 59 percent viewing their coursework as helpful. (See Figure 1.4.)

Both STEM and liberal arts majors were less likely to have positive perceptions of the life skills they had learned through their programs, and both perceived that they lacked the skills for their careers. Only 36 percent of traditional 18- to 24-year-old college-going learners felt they had the skills and knowledge to be successful in their careers.[45]

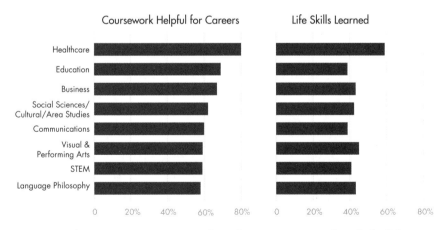

Figure 1.4 Few majors report that their coursework is helpful or that they acquired important life skills.

Source: Robot-Ready: Human+ Skills for the Future of Work. Emsi job posting analytics, 2018. © 2018, Strada Education Network.

Underemployment: Failure to Launch

Learners are more concerned and anxious than ever—and with good reason. We've all heard the stories of newly minted grads moving back into their parents' homes and working as baristas or selling clothes at a local retail outlet. This is the narrative of underemployment often conveyed through different media reporting, a phenomenon in which graduates get jobs that don't actually require college degrees. Even prior to the pandemic, there was evidence that graduates had already been struggling for years to get good jobs and accumulate wealth.[46]

Strada Institute worked with Burning Glass to analyze a sample of 4 million unique resumes. The longitudinal study revealed that with the exception of a few disciplines, such as engineering, computer science, and communications, college grads who started off underemployed had a higher likelihood of remaining underemployed five and ten years out.[47]

Forty-three percent of workers in the sample were underemployed in their first job, and they were five times more likely to remain so after five years than those who were not underemployed in their first job.[48] At the ten-year mark, close to 75 percent of workers who were underemployed as new graduates remained underemployed. These statistics show the persistence of the phenomenon—how underemployment is not a short-term problem and how the first job determines the quality of the second job, and the third job, and the fourth job. But if graduates were initially matched to a college-level job, approximately 90 percent of those individuals were able to avoid sliding into underemployment five and ten years later.

The risk of underemployment was lowest among most graduates in engineering and computer science, mathematics, and the physical sciences. In contrast, grads with degrees in security and law enforcement (65 percent), parks and recreation, leisure, and fitness studies (63 percent), and consumer and family sciences psychology (57 percent) had the highest levels of underemployment in their first job and were most at risk of being trapped in a permanent detour.

For women, the odds were significantly worse. Women were more likely to find themselves underemployed in their first job than men: 47 percent of female college graduates were initially underemployed, compared to 37 percent of male college graduates. With the exception of engineering—a field in which men and women were equally less likely to be underemployed—women faced higher rates of underemployment, no matter the discipline.

The first job also carried substantial financial implications with underemployed graduates earning on average $10,000 less annually than graduates working in college-level jobs. Of course, that number fails to take into account the compounding effects of graduates not being able to develop professional networks and social capital, or the social ties and personal connections that open doors to better opportunities.

The misalignment persists long after the initial handoff between education and work, which makes us wonder: If colleges and universities fail to launch graduates successfully the first time around, how in the world will they be able to support the 20 or 30 more job transitions to come?

2 The Theories Behind the End of College

In a 100-year work life, will we be going back to school? A public four-year education today can cost approximately $21,950 per year (including room and board), while a private nonprofit four-year college has skyrocketed to $49,870 per year (also including room and board).[1] With student debt ballooning to $1.6 trillion, far exceeding credit card debt, it seems hard to imagine that more college or more graduate school will be the answer in a longer work life.[2]

At the same time, the academic terrain has shifted dramatically over the years. In 1949, there were only 1,851 colleges in the United States (including both two- and four-year schools).[3] Since then, we've seen a vast proliferation of institutions of higher education as well as an increased number of learners enrolling in postsecondary education.[4] In 2012–2013, the number of universities peaked at 4,726 degree-granting institutions[5] with 70 percent of all graduating high schoolers enrolling in college.[6]

To fill those thousands of schools, there has to be a steady stream of learners coming through their doors to cover the rising cost of college. But the number of high school graduates peaked back in 2013. A Western Interstate Commission for Higher Education analysis revealed that the overall number of high school graduates will plateau over the next decade, leading to smaller college-graduating cohorts in the 2030s.[7] Indeed, in markets in the Northeast and Midwest, the number of high school grads started to stagnate and decline as early as 2010. This trend is a result of the declining number of white high schoolers. At first, the number is counterbalanced by the growth in Hispanic and Asian/Pacific Islander high school grads, but then the overall trend of decline continues, especially as private religious and nonsectarian schools are expected to graduate even fewer students.

By the mid-2030s, the projections look even starker. In certain graphs, there is a dramatic dip in enrollment. Gen Z, the generation born roughly between 1995 and 2010, will not meet the enrollment growth goals of most universities. Researcher Nathan Grawe describes this as the "birth dearth," the downward trend that is "a consequence of fertility declines that began during the financial crisis."[8]

Colleges and universities will no longer be able to rely on traditional demographics to fill their classrooms and residence halls. According to an analysis by the consulting company EY-Parthenon, over 100 institutions "exhibit more than four [of a possible eight] risk factors for closing," such as deficit spending, debt payments in excess of 10 percent of expenses, and enrollment under 1,000.[9] And that was pre-COVID.

In just the years between 2012 and 2018, various schools had already begun to merge, close, or create shared-services models to stay afloat. There had already been a noticeable contraction in the market with the number of degree-granting colleges and universities decreasing from over 4,700 institutions to 4,313.[10] With the coronavirus pandemic, the fate of schools is even more uncertain than ever, with Moody's Investors Service downgrading the 2020 outlook for higher education from stable to negative and early models estimating a 15 percent drop in enrollments nationwide.[11]

Adult Learners to the Rescue?

Amid all of this flux, the demographics of college-going students has been shifting over the last few decades. According to latest data from the National Center for Education Statistics, 4 in 10 college students are over the age of 24.[12] These learners do not live on campus; in fact, fewer than 2.7 million[13] students out of the nearly 20 million[14] who attend college in the United States go to school full-time and live on campus.

For years, we've been using the term "nontraditional" students, to contrast older and often part-time students with the younger 18- to 24-year-old student population that we tend to associate with residential college experiences. But "nontraditional" is a complete misnomer, as seven in ten students today display at least one of these nontraditional characteristics.[15] They're not necessarily coming to college for the social or coming-of-age experience—dorm life, partying, drinking, clubs, or sports. They are part-time students with full-time or multiple part-time work responsibilities. They have kids or other caregiving duties and may be tied to a geographic area because of these responsibilities. They have a lot of "life" that gets in the way and are seeking affordable and flexible learning pathways. They are less willing to pay for what they will never use. They are the new consumers of education.

The natural assumption might be: Given the decline in traditional college-going students, institutions would be delighted to discover this untapped market of millions more older adult learners. It seems almost too obvious to redesign solutions around this new population when the current market is shrinking.

But the inertia is substantial. Kevin Carey, vice president for education policy and knowledge management at New America Foundation, writes about this in his book *The End of College*. He quotes Harvard

biology professor Robert Lue, who explains that "higher education is
an organism. Our environment is changing, so we need to evolve. We
need to deconstrain, to redefine how our individual components relate
to one another. Organisms go extinct when they cannot mutate."[16]
Most colleges and universities are not mutating; they are neither
evolving their models nor tailoring their programs to attract and meet
the needs of this growing population of new learners.

For all of these reasons, many have been in the business of predict-
ing the disruption of college. Carey projects that schools will inevitably
struggle to compete with upstart innovators and organizations that
"take advantage of all those inefficiencies and drive the old business to
extinction."[17]

Disrupting College

Like harbingers of doom, observers have claimed that this company
or that start-up will undo higher education. The term "disruption" has
become one of the most overused buzzwords out there. There's an elegance to the word—an elegance that also, unfortunately, leads to its
broad misuse.

Clayton Christensen coined this term in his 1997 book *The
Innovator's Dilemma*.[18] He developed the idea of disruptive innovation
while studying for his doctoral business degree at Harvard. At a
basic level, he was trying to understand why it was so difficult for
major corporations and businesses to sustain success. How was it that
companies seemingly at the top of their game could collapse?

What Christensen discovered was the effect of innovations on the
margins, which could transform a product or service that used to be
very complicated and expensive, bring it to more people, improve it
over time, and ultimately upend an industry. The dynamic of disruption helps people understand why major industries and companies
have toppled over time—why, for instance, mini-mills disrupted

integrated mills in the steel industry. It helps describe why so many newspapers have gone out of print today and why we no longer buy music CDs. Disruption is a compelling phenomenon, and it can help us empathize with the kinds of business decisions that leaders face as they try to figure out how to sustain success.

A stronger grasp of disruption can help us dismantle our assumptions as we confront new ideas, innovations, and models that appear unusual or perhaps even make us feel threatened, uncomfortable, or scornful at first. Indeed, it is precisely when we feel tempted to dismiss a new model that we should probably start paying attention, because it might be just "good enough" (Christensen's words) to gain traction with people whose alternative is nothing at all. Christensen called this population *nonconsumers*, and it is ultimately through this lens of nonconsumers that we will find ways to ease our journey through a longer work life and make more obvious and seamless links between education and work.

The Pull of the Sustaining Trajectory

Imagine that you have a set of concentric circles. (See Figure 2.1.) The centermost circle describes the customers who have the most money or the most skills in that industry. The circles on the outer edges represent larger populations of the country who don't have as much money or as many skills. Almost always, modern industries start in that centermost

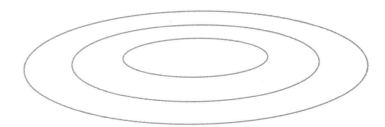

Figure 2.1 Populations of users.

circle because the first iterations of products are complicated and expensive. The first users, therefore, are the rare few with the skills and money to use the innovation.

Now, let's talk about the market in the context of that centermost circle. With most innovations, we witness improvements when it comes to the performance of a product or service over time. (See Figure 2.2.)

Some of the improvements that help companies move up this *sustaining* trajectory are just incremental changes from year to year, while others are dramatic, breakthrough innovations as companies pursue the creation of better and better products. The iPhone X or 11 are examples of products on a sustaining trajectory. Apple keeps making better and better versions of the iPhone for higher and higher price points.

But there's a second, concurrent trajectory to consider, and that is the ability for customers to absorb or leverage those performance boosts. Almost always, the trajectory of improvement outstrips the ability of customers to take advantage of that improvement. In the early 1980s, for example, the Intel 286 was the world's fastest chip, but it could barely keep pace with our fingertips as we engaged in simple

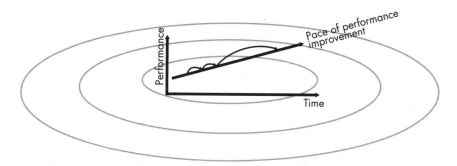

Figure 2.2 The first iterations of innovations are usually more complicated and expensive.

acts of word processing. We would type a sentence, pause, and watch the cursor catch up to our keystrokes.

That low end of performance is illustrated by the dotted line that sits over the solid line in the graph in Figure 2.3. Today, however, the processor in our laptops far exceeds our needs, as illustrated by the solid line hovering over the dotted line. Our computer processors now far outstrip our needs and what we're able to absorb as customers. We likely only take advantage of a small fraction of what those chips have to offer.

This trajectory of improvement is core to what we call *sustaining innovations*. And companies pursue sustaining innovations because this is what historically has helped them succeed. By charging the highest prices to their most demanding and sophisticated customers, companies achieve greater profitability. Almost always, the companies that lead sustaining innovations are the incumbent industry leaders because no matter how technologically difficult it is, if the innovation will allow companies to make better products to sell for better profits to their best customers, they will always figure out a way to get it done.

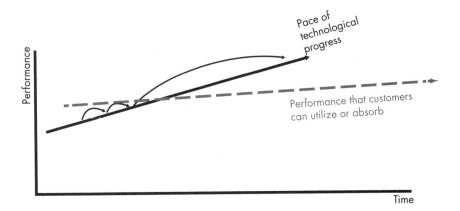

Figure 2.3 Two trajectories: The performance of a product or service over time and the improvements a user can absorb.

Disruption, however, is a countervailing set of innovations that drives prices down. A disruptive innovation transforms products and services that used to be complicated and expensive and makes them initially affordable and accessible to a whole new population of people, the nonconsumers.

What's a Nonconsumer?

Disruptive entrants never compete directly with an established market leader in that centermost circle, for the only way consumers will adopt that innovation is if it is demonstrably better than the incumbent's product in terms of quality and cost—an impossible feat for most entrants. Instead, disruptive entrants always start with an outer circle as their toehold—with the nonconsumers, or the people for whom the alternative is nothing at all.

As an example, the first personal computers (PCs) were marketed as children's toys and never as direct competition to mainframes or minicomputers. At $2,000 per unit as opposed to $2 million per unit, a different group of people was suddenly able to access an innovation previously out of reach. Children and hobbyists didn't care that the performance of the first PCs was underwhelming, to say the least; they were absolutely delighted by the quality of the computers, for they had nothing else with which to compare them.

Keenly aware of this new trend, Digital Equipment Corporation (DEC), one of the most admired minicomputing companies of the 1970s and 1980s, asked its customers if they needed PCs. But for the first ten years, the PC simply could not perform well enough for DEC's minicomputing customers, who needed better and more sophisticated minicomputers to help with controlling manufacturing processes or laboratory equipment, telecommunications, and early computer-aided design systems (CAD) work. These customers scoffed at the low quality of PCs, which meant that the more carefully DEC listened to its best customers, the fewer signals it got that the personal computer mattered—because it didn't matter at all to its customers.

The financial outlook for the company only confirmed for DEC's managers that they should cede this portion of the market. PC manufacturers were inhabiting the space deemed undesirable by established industry leaders. It simply did not make sense for DEC to pursue the PC market. DEC's gross margins were over $100,000 per minicomputer, whereas the gross margins that could be earned from selling a PC were less than $1,000 per unit. The choice for the management team was this: Should we make better products for our best customers for more profit, or should we alternatively ruin our margins by making computers that none of our customers desire?

The Innovator's Dilemma

Christensen called this choice *the innovator's dilemma* because it makes little to no economic or customer sense for successful organizations to pursue the bottom end of the market. In fact, it becomes far more attractive to cede that portion of the market to the new entrants in order to focus more deliberately on the sustaining trajectory.

Consider the perspective of the dominant Big Three car manufacturers in Michigan. American car makers were more than happy to cede the low end of the market to Toyota, which had just introduced the Corona, the first popular Toyota, in America in 1965. The Corona was a tiny car that broke down a bit too easily, but its first purchasers were not the same people who already owned cars or were seeking an upgrade. The company's target market were nonconsumers, people who were accustomed to walking or taking the bus. In those people's eyes, that somewhat crummy Corona was absolutely delightful compared to their alternative at the low end of the market: nothing at all.

Meanwhile, the Big Three found it much more appealing to create sustaining innovations—or bigger, better, and fancier cars for higher profit margins. The choice seemed obvious to them to produce more Cadillacs as opposed to cheaper (exploding) Pintos. What they did not anticipate, however, was that the disruptive entrant Toyota would improve its products over time to produce the Lexus brand and upend the incumbent Big Three.

This is true of almost all disruptive innovations. The companies entering from the margins start off as "good enough," but over time, they better understand what audiences need next in terms of performance, and they begin improving while moving upmarket to compete ultimately with those incumbent leaders.

This transformation, however, is not instantaneous. Disruption is a process, not an event. To illustrate, minimill technologies emerged as early as 1965, but integrated steel mills in North America really didn't start feeling the pain until the early 1990s, when the vast majority of them were forced to shutter their doors. And although the first PCs appeared in the late 1970s, DEC didn't collapse until 1989. Disruption doesn't happen overnight. It is a process that sometimes takes decades to come to fruition.

Disruption Starts with "Good Enough."   For higher education, it was only from the 1990s onward that a technological enabler—online technologies—became good enough for groups like University of Phoenix and DeVry University to consider moving upmarket by launching the first fully online universities. Now, two things generally occur when I mention these schools—both negative. Most people don't tend to think of University of Phoenix as a disruptive innovation because there's a sense that online education is an inferior educational offering that in no way can compete with the best schools. Others gasp at the mention of these for-profit colleges because they think of the stories about the worst for-profit actors fleecing the vulnerable, the working poor, and even homeless people across the nation.

Let's tackle the question of quality first. If we go back to the origin stories of Phoenix and DeVry, they first established themselves just as online technologies became reliable enough to help scale the teaching and learning process and cater to nonconsumers of higher education—students whose alternative to online higher education was no education at all. These entrants weren't competing on the same playing field as more traditional universities. By pushing into the outer rings (along the z-axis) to serve larger populations of learners with fewer resources, these first online entrants competed on an entirely different measure of quality (y-axis), to serve an entirely different market. (See Figure 2.4.)

When critics try to dismiss these learning pathways by disparaging the quality of these educational experiences, they miss the point that a disruptive innovation's first, simple application is often of lower quality according to traditional metrics of performance. They mistakenly scorn the offering as lower quality, but that's precisely the point. Generally, a disruptive entrant doesn't offer a breakthrough improvement, nor does it even offer a "good" product from the perspective of established organizations.

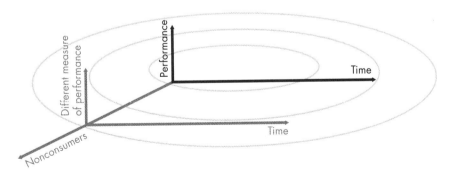

Figure 2.4 Disruptive innovations push out along the z-axis to touch larger populations of nonconsumers and therefore compete on a different measure of performance.

Despite the seeming inferiority of this new higher education "product," as well as higher tuition rates than what comparable public institutions charged for in-state students, nonconsumers flocked to these online universities. The measures of performance that mattered for these more mature working learners were flexibility and convenience. Bogged down by various commitments like work and family, these learners viewed commuting to a campus as impossible and the opportunity cost of pursuing education, or the cost of forgone wages, simply too high. But an option that allowed them to continue working and skill up? Now, that was compelling.

Sadly, however, these universities were never able to shift from those outer rings and improve their experiences in order to move upmarket. Instead, leading for-profit universities got caught gaming the federal financial aid system, leveraging predatory recruiting practices to the point where the number of enrollments ballooned to 2,022,785 learners in 2010—many of whom were leaving with debt and no degree.[19]

In a scathing report, the 2012 Senate majority cracked down on bad actors in the for-profit education space. But in that same report was an acknowledgment that these schools—in theory—were positioned to play an "important role in higher education" for "'a new majority' of non-traditional students": "They offer the convenience of nearby campus and online locations, a structured approach to coursework and flexibility to stop and start classes quickly and easily. These innovations have made attending college a viable option for many working adults, and have proven successful for hundreds of thousands of people who might not otherwise have obtained degrees."[20] In other words, early for-profits started out well equipped to cater to nonconsumers but then lost their way.

Mission Focus in the Midst of Mission Creep. Taking a cue from the early for-profits, Southern New Hampshire University (SNHU),

Western Governors University (WGU), BYU-Pathway World-wide, and Arizona State University (ASU)—all with a heavy online presence—emerged as another wave of innovators. And just like Phoenix and DeVry, these schools have focused on the singular value proposition of teaching the new majority of learners—Christensen's nonconsumers.

Most have done away with tenure, committees, and research and, at the same time, have subdivided the teacher's role so that the person teaching the online course is separate from the person evaluating student work for grades. These instructors are also different from the people responsible for coaching and mentoring students along in their academic careers. WGU, as an example, features student mentors, course mentors, and evaluators. In other programs, there are lead faculty, subject-matter experts, assessors, tutors, mentors, and coaches.

This is an especially interesting tack, as over the last few decades, the rest of higher education has been marked by sustaining inno-vations. In an effort to outpace fellow institutions in the game of college rankings, schools have improved classrooms, built more buildings, updated technology, sponsored faculty research, increased administrative overhead, and decked out residence halls and dining facilities. As a report from the National Bureau of Economic Research explains, "For many institutions, demand-side market pressure may not compel investment in academic quality, but rather in consumption amenities."[21]

There are various labels for this upmarket pull in higher education. Economist Gordon Winston describes it as an "arms race."[22] Kaplan CEO Andrew Rosen calls it "Harvard envy": the desire of universities to emulate Harvard's prestige and exclusivity by "spending far too much time and energy trying to be something they're not."[23] Phil Regier, CEO of EdPlus at ASU, describes the pull of isomorphism as if it were the Iditarod: "Universities tend to be lined up very much like sled dogs, where in my academic discipline, we were chasing University of Texas, which was chasing the University of Michigan, which wanted to be like Northwestern, which really wanted to be like Harvard. They were just lined up."[24]

Academic Inertia. The allure of creating more sustaining innovations is so intense because, like most businesses, colleges are comprised of four basic and deeply interdependent components, as shown in Figure 2.5.

The starting point in the creation of any successful organization's business model is its value proposition. For a liberal arts college, for instance, that priority might be to offer excellent teaching in small, intimate settings. Institutional leaders then put into play resources and processes to deliver that value proposition.

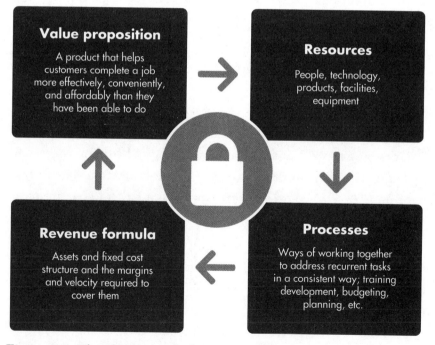

Figure 2.5 The elements of a business model.

Source: Reprinted from Michelle R. Weise and Clayton Christensen, Hire Education: Mastery, Modularization, and the Workforce Revolution. © 2014, Clayton Christensen Institute.

In the case of a small liberal arts college, resources include faculty members in different departments, dollars spent per student, buildings, labs, and other capital expenditures. Processes such as course enrollment, student recruitment, financial aid packaging, tenure promotion, accreditation management, and fundraising coalesce to define how resources are combined to deliver the value proposition. This very complex set of elements goes through multiple iterations and cycles of change before a stable revenue formula emerges, which also depends on state and federal subsidies, tuition, and endowment funds.

The right balance is difficult to achieve. In fact, once the four interdependent components come together to deliver education in a sustainable manner, the business model then begins to work in reverse. Instead of the value proposition driving the resources, processes, and revenue formula, the business model begins to dictate the sorts of value propositions the organization can or cannot deliver.[25] Because this balance is so challenging to get right, the business model of traditional institutions cannot evolve easily, particularly in the face of rapid innovation.

These same dynamics are at work in every company and every organization. The powerful forces that emerge from the balancing act of Figure 2.5 inevitably take every new innovative proposal and shape it into a sustaining innovation, or one that conforms to the existing business model. This is a core reason why traditional institutions are at a disadvantage when disruptive innovations emerge as well as why most are not pivoting to serve more adult learners. Schools are motivated to pursue sustaining innovations and invest in improvements that affect only their existing or most desirable and demanding customers. Disruptive innovations generally appear unattractive to a traditional institution, since the innovations are fundamentally at odds with the college's value proposition, resources, processes, and revenue formula.[26]

To complicate matters, most universities offer *three* distinct and often conflicting value propositions around knowledge creation (research), knowledge proliferation (teaching), and preparation for life and careers (social growth)—all bundled together under the auspices of a single brick-and-mortar institution.[27] The existing business model is constrained three times over. When I spoke at an event in 2017 about these conflicting business models, a senior leader handling finances for Stanford University raised his hand and said, "Michelle, we don't have three; we have 17," and went on to list hospitals, land, and multiple other business models.

Can You Disrupt from Within?

Given this complexity and the resulting inertia, many of the new wave of online universities I mentioned earlier are looking to Christensen's theories as a playbook for innovation. In *The Innovator's Dilemma,* Christensen makes the case for housing nascent initiatives in separate, autonomous entities with "an unfettered charter to build a completely new business with a completely new business model."[28]

IBM succeeded in doing this, in contrast to its competitor DEC, during the first five years of the development of personal computing.[29] IBM had cleverly set up a PC unit in Florida—separate from its mainframe and minicomputer business units in New York and Minnesota. But geographical distance was not the point; instead, the critical factor was that the leaders at IBM empowered the new tiger team for PCs to develop a new business model and culture completely distinct from the business model of minicomputers, the dominant product at the time. They freed the team from the habits and culture of the existing organization and the way things had always been done. Instead, the tiger team could explore new models that depended on low margins, low overhead costs, and high unit volume.

Autonomous Growth Units for Higher Ed. In the same vein, innovators in online education are prototyping new structures to catalyze growth in new markets by allowing experimental and independent labs to play by different rules and foster values and processes different from the incumbent model.

Paul LeBlanc, president of SNHU, introduced some basic rules of decentralization informed by Clay's research, including "room to play by different rules, finding underserved markets, clarity about the job we are doing."[30] He described these moves as a way to "negotiate some breathing room" among the different entities as well as their governance structures—that separation is critical in allowing the new thing to prove itself and to figure out the new business model.

None of this, however, was easy. Each time LeBlanc tried to create a new unit, the recurring reaction was a strong desire on the part of the incumbent model to take on the new initiative rather than spawn a separate, autonomous unit:

> So, the folks at Online often thank me for buffering them from the main campus and giving them room to grow. . . . When we launched the Innovation Lab and College for America, [Online] wanted to own that. "We can do that! We know that world. We know that market." And I said, "No, not really. We're going to do something a little different over here." So the same phenomenon that was happening on the main campus where the main campus was trying to pull [Online] back to re-create them in their own image, they were trying to do that with the Innovation Lab/College for America. . . . It's not ill-intended or from a bad place; it is just the inherent propensity of the incumbent to want to own the new and to make the new play by the incumbent's rules and way of seeing the world.

LeBlanc likened this propensity to a human body's predisposition to raise its defenses against any new entrant as if it were foreign tissue. "It plays out over and over and over again," he said, "and it has nothing to do with good or bad ideas or smart or not smart thinking—it's the larger cultural and organizational dynamic of incumbents and new foreign 'tissue.'"

Scott Pulsipher, the president of WGU, described the very same phenomenon in his efforts to separate lines of work with sufficient breathing room: "I, even as the senior executive, fought my own staff about [WGU Academies]. . . . But what is the operating impera- tive? What is the design? What are the outcomes of that? How do you measure success and such? And if it is decidedly different than a university . . . it gets really hard to innovate within the existing imperative."[31]

These presidents are pushing the boundaries of transformation from within a university setting. And their enablement of autonomous growth units appears to be working. Many online "mega-universities" are increasing their enrollment numbers in dramatic fashion, with some hovering over 100,000 (primarily adult) learners per year.[32]

But Are These Autonomous Growth Strategies Disruptive?

Not necessarily. Most schools are still building degree programs that are tethered to the existing value network of accreditation. What that means is that these initiatives are all still tied to the values, pro- cesses, and regulations that govern sustaining innovations. Accreditors are the imperfect agencies that serve as the gatekeepers of Title IV student aid, the primary form of federal support for colleges and universities.[33]

As Christensen, Michael Horn, and Curtis Johnson assert in *Dis- rupting Class*, "It is important not to regulate disruptive innovations with the old regulatory scheme where they won't perform as well and where we risk the danger of consigning the disruptive innovations to looking like the old system."[34] For all of the innovation, many of these newer programs are not exactly creating a new value network but rather functioning as new light bulbs in old sockets.

Disruptive products require disruptive channels.[35] And developing disruptive channels has been one of the toughest nuts to crack for even the most innovative postsecondary education providers.

Christensen and I wrote about the opportunities for disruption in higher education back in 2014 in a book called *Hire Education: Mastery, Modularization, and the Workforce Revolution*.[36] At the time, journalists, pundits, and observers kept asking the Christensen Institute to comment on whether massive open online courses (MOOCs) were disruptive. We instead pointed to something called online competency-based education (CBE) aligned to workforce needs, which we found to be flying under the radar and much more interesting. The promise of online CBE was to smooth the transition between education and work and to make clear to employers what learners could *do* with their knowledge.

Fixed Student Learning Outcomes

Most institutions of higher education measure learning in credit hours, meaning that they're very good at telling you how long a student sat in a particular class but not what the student actually learned. Timing is fixed, and learning can be variable. College transcripts ultimately reveal very little about what a student knows and can do. An employer never fully knows what it means if a student got a B+ in social anthropology or a C- in geology. Even a report from the Carnegie Foundation acknowledged that the credit hour, also known as the Carnegie unit, was "miscast as a measure of student learning."[37]

Competency-based learning flips time-based learning on its head and centers on mastery of a subject regardless of the time it takes to get there. A student cannot move on until demonstrating proficiency or fluency. Learning is fixed, and time is variable.

Competencies alone are nothing new; schools have been delivering CBE in face-to-face programs for decades. But Christensen and I identified the possibility of moving toward more disruptive models in postsecondary education by combining competency- or mastery-based learning, modularization, and the creation of a new value network outside of accreditation. And early innovations seemed to be ticking the boxes in terms of a critical convergence of multiple vectors: the right learning model, the right technologies, the right customers, and the right business models.

The Unfulfilled Promise of Competency-Based Education

After we wrote our book, the field was abuzz with reports that over 600 colleges were experimenting with CBE.[38] Unfortunately, the initial enthusiasm for CBE led to hundreds of colleges mistakenly viewing the creation of competencies as the secret sauce for success.

Operating in silos, every college began developing its own proprietary skills taxonomy rather than working together toward a common language. We now quite possibly have hundreds or thousands of competencies that all mean the same thing but do not carry meaning across institutional, state, or employer boundaries. In their focus on translating college credits into competencies, learning providers also neglected to consider the two other key markers of disruption: modularization and the creation of a new value network of employers.

Modularization. As significant as mastery-based learning is compared to our time-based system, Christensen and I made clear that it was the fusion of CBE with online technologies that was groundbreaking because it could lead to more modularized learning.

Modularity breaks up learning into units that can be studied as stand-alone modules and in whatever sequence the learner needs. At the same time, learning providers can more cost-effectively combine modules of learning into pathways that are agile and adaptable to the changing labor market.

Think discrete Lego pieces: Competencies have a unique architecture because they are not tethered to specific courses but are instead composed of a series of learning objectives or can-do statements: This learner can create a research-based argument, for instance; this learner can use appropriate mathematical formulas to inform financial decisions; or this learner can speak effectively in order to persuade or motivate. So, the same module can be deployed in a variety of settings: A student in an MBA program and another student in a nursing program might have similar learning objectives but draw on different content and materials to achieve those objectives and demonstrate that competency.

By breaking free of the constraints of the "course" as the educational unit, an online CBE provider can combine and stack learning modules together in different ways for various students. Using the same pieces, a Lego bridge becomes a Lego house.

In late 2014, MIT created an institute-wide task force on the future of undergraduate education that homed in on this specific architecture and the need for modularization whenever possible: "The very notion of a 'class' may be outdated. This in many ways mirrors the preferences of students on campus. The unbundling of classes also reflects a larger trend in society—a number of other media offerings have become available in modules, whether it is a song from an album, an article in a newspaper, or a chapter from a textbook. Modularity also enables 'just-in-time' delivery of instruction, further enabling project-based learning on campus and for students worldwide."[39] Nowhere else but in an online competency-based curriculum will you find this novel and flexible architecture, which can help businesses and organizations of all sizes skill up their existing workforce for new and emerging roles.

The Mythical, Stackable Credential. To date, however, we have not seen learning providers take full advantage of what competencies have to offer through modularization. Instead, most of the innovation has been channeled into degree programs or *stackable* credentials that lead to a degree.

Education providers tend to assume that every learner would like to stack learning toward a degree because a bachelor's degree is one of the surest bets to conferring greater lifetime earnings and enabling access to jobs with family-sustaining wages.[40] The idea behind a stackable credential is that a degree may feel daunting for someone who is juggling multiple responsibilities as a working learner; by snapping together smaller bits of learning, a person can celebrate small wins along the longer path to a degree.

But simply dividing up a degree program into smaller, bite-size chunks will not suffice. President Clark Gilbert of Brigham Young University–Pathway, a spin-out of BYU and BYU–Idaho, explained in an interview that it took an incredible amount of effort to launch a novel certificate-first approach and reengineer the "degree structure so there's value in the first year—not just prerequisites":

> What we actually have found is: when students complete a job skill certificate, the odds they keep going toward the bachelor's degree go up by 25 points. I mean, it's our best retention program . . . more than scholarshipping, more than mentoring. It is to have something tangible that led to a job because then, at-risk populations realize, "Oh my goodness. Education pays," and then . . . after they get their first job, they will keep going online and finish their degree.[41]

Now the school's 50,000 students in 100 different countries can acquire a job skill first that "has value on the job market." These include lucrative certificates in areas like diesel mechanics, where learners are earning up to $90,000 per year en route to attaining an associate or bachelor's degree. Not only do these certificates lead to good jobs, but they also increase persistence in longer programs.

But, in general, more of the innovation in microcredentials actually has been occurring in the space *beyond* a bachelor's degree. Programs such as MicroMasters at edX and Specializations at Coursera are mostly attracting well-educated populations—not to mention mostly white or Asian learners with degrees who are already employed.[42] Moreover, the microcredentials appear to lack work relevance: Of the few who actually completed microcredentials beyond a bachelor's degree, a mere 6 percent said that the program helped them get a pay raise.[43]

"There's a lot of work still to do if we want microcredentials and MOOCs to emerge as an alternative to an undergraduate degree and also to serve a more historically disadvantaged population that has not had access to the institutions that are providing these offerings," explains Sean Gallagher, executive director of Northeastern University's Center for the Future of Higher Education and Talent Strategy.[44]

The New Consumers.   Christensen's concept of nonconsumers reminds us to return to the people whose alternative is nothing at all in order to identify the skills we need to build, the pathways we need to design, and the funding mechanisms that we need to foster. A bundle of modules doesn't always need to culminate in a credential or a degree. The new education consumers may not even be looking for a degree. They may be seeking targeted programs that can be completed in a short time frame to reduce time away from paid work and get them into new jobs quickly.

They are turning to postsecondary education for a very specific reason. Pew Research reveals that 87 percent of adults in the workforce today acknowledge that it will be essential or important for them to get training and develop new skills throughout their work lives.[45] At the same time, however, they cannot necessarily fathom returning to traditional education pathways because they weren't successful there the first time around.

Community college statistics bring this problem into sharp relief. Federal statistics show that only 27 percent[46] of first-time, full-time students earn an associate degree within three years and only one in five moves on to earn a bachelor's degree in six years.[47] Millions of Americans never *complete* their degrees.

For many years, policymakers and leaders in higher education tried to lure this particular population back to school to complete their degrees and advance their work lives. The effort has not been as successful as imagined. In a large-scale survey, Strada and Gallup took a close look at 44,777 adults in this some-college-no-degree population, and 56 percent of respondents confirmed that they had no intention of returning to pursue a college education.[48] They explained that they were not willing to go back to school even though they *knew* that a degree could help them advance their careers.

Workers' lack of interest in returning to college is primarily driven by cost barriers and time to degree, but they have also lost faith in higher education as the place to go to reskill and upskill throughout their lives in order to adapt to the jobs of the future, according to another Gallup survey with Northeastern.[49] Only 22 percent of adults agree that colleges and universities are adequately preparing students for future jobs involving technology. More than 40 percent of workers also believe that college programs don't keep up with the job market—that prerequisites and course schedules aren't flexible enough and that the learning isn't as hands-on as it should be.

The new working learner is a different kind of consumer of education and will seek pathways that are more agile and more adaptable to changing labor market needs. The disruptive entrants of the future will have to engage with these learners differently from before and offer more convenient, targeted, and personalized pathways.

Everything Before the Degree. The new consumers of education are seeking more direct connections to good work. They also want to be sure that whatever path they select, those new skills will signal something meaningful to a future employer. That endorsement, more than anything, will be the validation they seek.

In the space of everything *before* the bachelor's degree, learning providers have the opportunity to develop true stand-alone modules of learning and narrow in on a particular person's skills gap in ways that traditional forms of postsecondary education cannot duplicate.

Maybe a learner only needs four, 11, or whatever the number may be of brief modules to skill up and advance. The flexible architecture of modularized competencies, which technology enhances, allows providers to create and scale a multitude of stackable credentials or programs for a wide variety of industries. At the same time, learning providers can personalize pathways that flex with the busy lives of very different consumers of education.

A New Value Network of Employers. But education and training providers will have to be deliberate about bypassing the system of accreditation. Because employers are the ultimate consumer of the graduates in training—not accreditors—employers are the ones who need to be persuaded. By creating a separate and compelling value network comprised of employers, these more modularized programs have the power to validate pathways without having to seek accreditation.

This approach works especially well for emerging fields, such as data science, logistics, or cloud management, or other subjects not traditionally taught in colleges and universities. Learning providers could collaborate directly with employers to determine the competencies required to build streamlined, hands-on learning pathways. At the same time, employers could test and validate these newer types of learning experiences as active participants in the coordination and creation of those competencies.

There is a $655 billion industry—60 percent of the total $1.1 trillion being spent on postsecondary education in the United States—devoted to industry training and certification.[50] This funding stream includes employer-provided formal training ($177 billion), employer-provided informal training ($413 billion), certifications, apprenticeships and other workforce training ($47 billion), and public job training ($18 billion).

There is enormous room for innovation in the marketplace of portable and stackable credentials to prove what it is that a person knows and can do. More direct collaborations or employer-validated learning experiences have the potential to create a separate and possibly even more powerful value network that supersedes the signaling effect of a degree.

3 The Future of Workers, the Future of Us

Academic or institutional inertia is a real, palpable force to be reckoned with, but there's just as much complexity to be found within the workforce. It's not just that the education infrastructure has failed to keep pace with tech's transformation of the economy, as corporate leaders are prone to suggest. The onus is on companies just as much as it is on higher education to respond more rapidly and urgently to the changing nature of work.

The Blame Game: Send in the Employers

Over the last few decades in particular, employers have retreated from training their people as they used to, creating a reskilling crisis in America. "Companies simply haven't invested much in training their workers," says Peter Cappelli, director of Wharton's Center for Human Resources.[1] In his analysis, he shows how in 1979, young workers got an average of 2.5 weeks of training per year and by 1995, the average amount of training workers received per year was just under 11 hours, with workplace safety ranked as the most common topic.

Few people—only about a fifth of employees, according to Accenture—report getting on-the-job training from their employers.[2] And when they do, that training falls under compliance training or risk mitigation for the employer; it's not about building new skills.

It wasn't always this way. Cappelli explains that companies used to grow talent from within: "[C]orporations filled roughly 90% of their vacancies through promotions and lateral assignments between the end of World War II and the 1970s. Today, that figure is one third or less."[3] When asked why this is the case, 72 percent of corporations report that they don't view internal staff as strong candidates for vacancies. Cappelli has a different interpretation of all the numbers: "What employers really want are workers they don't have to train."

Indeed, business leaders are more prone to hire machines over people.[4] A 2013 Harvard Business School survey revealed that most business leaders prefer to invest in technology rather than overhaul complex human capital management chains or negotiate all of the challenges that come with reskilling workers and talent development.[5]

Or, faced with the question of whether to "buy or build" talent, the reflex of most employers has been to buy and look externally for new talent rather than offer reskilling opportunities in-house. Coding bootcamp founder Jake Schwartz has called it the "corporate hunger games of recruiting and replacing talent."[6]

The situation became instantly bleaker when the 2020 global pandemic hit and forced millions of Americans, especially those in retail or hospitality jobs, to pivot to entirely new fields in search of employment. Pre-COVID-19, it was hard enough for workers to progress in a linear fashion, or from role to role in a specific occupation or field. Businesses had not been engaging their existing employee base to address new and emerging forms of work. So to suddenly shift and somehow help newly laid-off or furloughed workers translate and transfer their skills to better-paying and more stable jobs in altogether different fields? It was a totally foreign concept.

The coronavirus laid bare the prolonged lack of investment in talent development. Despite the fact that nearly all CEOs (93 percent) recognize "the need to change their strategy for attracting and retaining talent," a whopping 61 percent have never even taken the first step.[7] Business leaders have been consistently missing out on the strategic need to accelerate a new and transformative human capital development agenda for the work of the future. And now, that future is our present of work.

The Caring Economy

To complicate matters, employers will have to brace for major fluctuations in their talent pools, especially as their workers get older, stay in the workforce longer, and simultaneously have to care for a growing graying population. In the future, it is inevitable that more employees will have to shoulder more personal caregiving responsibilities. There will be more aging and elderly people to take care of who will likely endure more chronic health issues as their lives extend longer than those of our predecessors. It is therefore no surprise that one of the areas with the largest projected growth in jobs is home health aide work.[8]

Today, as many as 73 percent of employees already report having some type of current caregiving responsibility, reports Harvard Business School professor Joseph Fuller.[9] "Already, the average American family caregiver spends roughly 24 hours per week providing care; one in four spends more than 40 hours a week on caregiving responsibilities." It's just been hidden from view, but a great majority of our workforce engages in unpaid work in caring for children, disabled and sick children, and elders—many of whom have illnesses, injuries, and disabilities. These responsibilities are so extensive and time-consuming that one out of three employees must voluntarily leave paid work to engage in caregiving activities.

Current workplaces do not flex and make way for this new normal. In our research at Strada Institute for the Future of Work, one man whom we interviewed who is still looking for work in his 60s described the challenges of having to take care of his mother who has been seriously ill for eight months. He explained how it has taken him away from his job search: "I've noticed people that end up in a situation, where they're helping somebody or caring for somebody, have difficulty getting restarted . . . maybe it's just really hard to get the momentum back, I think."[10] Unfortunately, standard-length workdays do not allow for the growing need to scale back or opt into and out of work because of caregiving responsibilities.

The demographic changes to come, however, mean that the burdens of caregiving will only increase and intensify, and companies will have to create better paths to reentry for employees balancing work and these major responsibilities. It will be critical for employers to think deliberately about how to build more on- and off-ramps in and out of work.

Let's Not Forget Our 50+ Workers

Companies will not only need to diversify their ways of developing, supporting, and retaining talent, but they will also have to figure out how to pull more talent from the fastest-growing portion of our population: workers over the age of 50. We cannot talk about long-life learning without discussing the often-forgotten source of some of our greatest human capital.

In the United States, older, retirement-age people, known as the silver generation, are making up a larger share of our overall citizenry. According to the Pew Research Center, in 2014 there were 75 million baby boomers age 51 to 69.[11] Census Bureau data suggests that those numbers will rise sharply, to the point where the share of seniors over 65 will match the shares of people ages 25 to 44 and 45 to 64.[12]

More mature workers are already extending their stays in the workforce. The percentage of Americans planning to work past age 65 has increased from 16 percent in 1991 to 48 percent in 2018. With pensions having largely disappeared and funding insufficient for most people to sustain more years after retirement, more workers are planning on *never* retiring.[13]

American public and private pension systems were not set up for a longer life and are currently underfunded to pay their promised benefits. With much lower employment among those age 65 and over, the aging of the population will pose fundamental public policy challenges, as the "dependency ratio"—the ratio of nonworkers to workers—rises sharply and labor force growth slows.

Under current law and tax rates, Social Security is projected to cover only approximately 75 percent of its promised benefits through 2094. The latest estimate is that the Social Security Trust Fund will be depleted in 2034 or 2035, at which point payments to retirees will be cut by 20 percent across the board and by 25 percent soon after.[14] Taken together, it is clear that, as a nation, we have not saved enough—whether publicly or privately—to pay for the retirement benefits we have promised to those who will retire over the next decades.

Employers will have to embrace a starkly different approach. To reduce the stress on these public and private systems, workers over the age of 50 must be empowered to bridge a looming retirement shortfall by earning and saving more, thus spending fewer years dependent on their retirement savings. As a report by the Organization for Economic Cooperation and Development (OECD) states, "We need workers who want to work longer, but also employers who want to employ them."[15]

Companies are not accustomed to engaging with a more mature worker, as 50+ employees are well aware. One interviewee in her 60s explained, "You have the most pay; you have the most benefits. That's who they want to get rid of . . . . And people would say, 'Oh, they're not going to lay you off. You've been there 29 years.' And I said, 'Yeah, they're going to lay me off *because* I've been there 29 years.'" One man in his late 60s speculated, "Some people maybe view that if you're in the same position for too long, that you're not growing. That may be a negative in terms of your employability."

Hiring managers may assume that older job seekers' skills are out of date for today's opportunities, especially when compared to more recent graduates. Or, they may just assume that a 50+ worker will always be more expensive and potentially harder to train than a younger person. Indeed, workers in their 50s often command the highest wages of their lifetimes. Across OECD countries, every extra decade on the job is estimated to add 6 percent to wages.[16] Someone who starts working at the age of 25 and receives 3 percent annual pay raises by age 55 will be earning 2.4 times what the novice 25-year-old earns and twice as much as a 32-year-old. It's therefore tempting for employers to perceive younger workers as a cheaper investment.[17]

Or, hiring managers may not even be aware of the role age (or other factors) plays in their analysis. Bias, whether implicit or explicit, usually infiltrates the interviewing and decision-making process.[18] One major study set out to show how challenging it is for older people to attain even low-level jobs. Researchers David Neumark, Ian Burn, and Patrick Button used technology to send out what they described as "triplets of otherwise identical young, middle-aged, and older fictitious applications to over 13,000 positions in 12 cities spread across 11 states, totaling more than 40,000 applicants—by far the largest scale audit or correspondence study to date."[19]

The study focused on what the researchers called low-skilled jobs—administrative assistants, janitors, security guards, and retail sales—but all of the applications were identical except that the profiles were young (ages 29 to 31), middle age (ages 49 to 51), or older (ages 64 to 66).[20] It found that both middle-age and older applicants received fewer callbacks, but the oldest applicants experienced the most discrimination. Moreover, middle-age and older women experienced more age discrimination than men of those ages. Differences in callback rates for older women relative to younger women ranged as high as 47 percent.[21] The authors proved that "age discrimination makes it harder for older individuals, especially women, to get hired into new jobs."[22]

Older workers need a fair shot to be contenders in the workforce of the future. In France, the Public Employment service is using aptitude testing as a way to select candidates for employer interviews in order to combat age bias.[23] U.S. labor law, however, prohibits the use of competency-based assessments as the sole determinant for hiring.[24] Nevertheless, companies need new techniques to mitigate against current pitfalls in hiring.

Mature workers—arguably even more than younger workers—need validation or endorsement of the skills they've developed, either through their experience in the same or other industries or through training or education they have obtained. They will need fair ways of signaling their aptitude and disposition for success now and in the future and of proving that they are open to new technologies and possess sought-after skills like empathy and situational wisdom.

In a world where less human labor—especially of the traditional physical sort—will be required for the work ahead, more mature workers represent a deep pool of experienced human capital, a critical source of the human skills employers so desperately seek.[25]

What Got Us Here Won't Get Us There

Both educators and employers are missing the mark. Employers are retreating from training, and our education infrastructure is lagging behind an economy transforming at an exponential pace. There is also a lack of a common language around skills. There are issues with funding as well, with continuing cutbacks of government support for higher education and slashing of state appropriations for postsecondary programs and workforce development efforts. Meanwhile, millions of Americans can't access good jobs or good wages.

None of this, however, occurred overnight or because of a global pandemic. The disconnect between people and better economic opportunity is the product of new technologies, competitive pressures, policy shifts, and changing employer and job seeker mindsets, exacerbated by the limited evolution of the way we train and hire workers. All of these challenges and more are occurring at once, and the seemingly intractable problems we face today are mired in a complex tangle.

Strangely, however, businesses, funders, investors, policymakers, and innovators continue to view these problems through silos. American philosopher and activist Marilyn Frye describes this phenomenon as a birdcage problem, a kind of stakeholder myopia:

> If you look very closely at just one wire in the cage, you cannot see the other wires. . . . It is only when you step back, stop looking at the wires one by one, microscopically, and take a macroscopic view of the whole cage, that you can see why the bird does not go anywhere; and then you will see it in a moment . . . the bird is surrounded by a network of systematically related barriers, no one of which would be the least hindrance to its flight, but which, by their relations to each other, are as confining as the solid walls of a dungeon.[26]

In this complex intersection between education and work, we typically talk about our system of K–12 education, which is usually separated from our system of higher education, which, in turn, is walled off from our workforce training system. But we need a more holistic approach that acknowledges the complexity of this network of systematically related barriers and deep form of interdependence.

Not Systems, But an Ecosystem

It's becoming clear that we're facing more of an ecosystem challenge. Ecosystems are complex and evolving—a community or network of interconnected, interacting organisms.

Recasting our education-to-and-through-employment system as an ecosystem better reflects the necessary interdependence of stakeholders in the system (learners, employers, education providers, governments, and more) with their environments (natural, technological, economic, cultural) and the dynamics of change within this web of interconnected living and nonliving things. It includes public, nonprofit, and proprietary schools across the student life cycle. It is enabled by a multiplicity of financing solutions, content, software, hardware, data, and infrastructure. The ecosystem is affected by a multitude of interest groups, often with competing missions, theories of action, and relationships to policy.

This interdependence is what makes change so complex and difficult to achieve. In *The Water of Systems Change*, John Kania and his coauthors explain how most complex ecosystem problems involve different types of interconnected conditions—structural, semiexplicit, and transformative—that keep a problem in place.[27] These conditions include policies, practices, resource flows, relationships and connections, power dynamics, and mental models.

The ecosystem cannot be fixed by cutting one or more of these stakeholders out of the equation or by putting the onus on higher education or employers to find a solution. Nor will these problems be mended overnight by a single organization throwing money at the problem. One centralized response will not meet the demands of a diverse range of learners and workers in various geographies and industries. It's much more complicated and interdependent than that.

In an ecosystem, we have to think about growth or thriving as it relates not only to the sum total of resources but also to the scarcest resource, the limiting factor. An ecosystem grows and thrives by the health of its limiting factors. And in our particular value chain made up of millions of educators, learners, and employers and layers of federal, state, and local policies, the most critical contingent we must pay attention to are the people who are being left behind.

We are all connected, and if a large contingent of our citizenry is not thriving today, that affects and touches every other stakeholder in the ecosystem. By centering on and designing toward the needs of those who are struggling the most, we can identify and solve for the pain points, barriers, and frictions that make a healthy and functioning learn-and-work ecosystem impossible today.

The Opportunity Gap

The future is already here—it's just not evenly distributed yet.

—William Gibson[28]

Even as we debate what the future of work will look like, it has already arrived. "To know about the future of work," explains Byron Auguste, former deputy director of the White House National Economic Council, "the most important thing to understand is the present of work and the challenges that people already face. More than a skills gap, we have an opportunity gap."[29]

Long before the 2020 global pandemic, COVID-19, we were facing an already dire problem of social (im)mobility for our most vulnerable citizens. Globally, the top 10 percent in OECD countries had been earning ten times more than the bottom 10 percent.[30] In the United States, widening inequality started as early as 1979, and the gains of the wealthiest Americans have since grown four times as fast as those of the bottom 10 percent of the population.[31]

America is, as Oren Cass from the Manhattan Institute explains, "at once booming and fading."[32] Americans have witnessed their incomes fall or remain flat while the cost of education, health care, and housing has continued to rise. Working-class adults, in particular, or folks who are working age (25 to 64) and in the lowest quartile in terms of earnings, income, and educational attainment, have been disproportionately hurt by automation and globalization.[33] They have endured massive job losses and downward pressure on wages in the careers and industries in which they have worked.

After the 2008 recession, the people who captured nearly all of the job growth in the postrecession economic recovery were workers with at least some education or training beyond high school; only 400,000 of the 18.3 million jobs created went to those with no college education.[34] Now adults with only a high school diploma are 50 percent more likely to live in poverty than those with some college or a two-year degree.[35] And, sadly, those educational and economic prospects are being passed on to children; only two out of every 25 children born into low-income households will ever reach the top rungs of the economic ladder.[36]

The term "working class" often conjures an image of a white, male, blue-collar worker, when, in reality, working-class adults comprise an incredibly diverse population in terms of race, ethnicity, families, and life experience. They are also a massive part of our ecosystem. Prior to the pandemic, there were already over 41 million Americans struggling to earn a living wage in the labor market.[37]

For millions of people, it can feel nearly impossible to move ahead. "Workers are losing their jobs and their social supports," write the authors of the report *Work, Skills, Community*, "and with them, in many cases, their sense of their identity and their place in the world."[38] For every 100 working-class adults, 47 are jobless; 15 are working part-time, and 38 are working full-time. Of those who are jobless, many have been forced to retire because their employer has pushed them out, or they have had to leave due to declining health, especially adults over the age of 50.[39] Many other jobless adults have completely lost confidence in their ability to find a job. After being unemployed for six months or a year, they give up looking for work.[40]

Without a connection to regular work and the dignity, self-respect, and empowerment it brings with it, the loss of purpose can be profound. In their joint research, Anne Case and Angus Deaton have revealed jaw-dropping data about "deaths of despair" brought on by opioid and alcohol abuse, suicide, and general distress, anxiety, and hopelessness.[41] For white and black people without a college degree—across the age spectrum—the death rates have surged.[42]

Mortality in the United States is moving in the exact opposite direction as in the rest of the world. The global population is living longer while life expectancy in the United States has consistently fallen since 2014 due to more drug overdoses, alcohol abuse, suicides, and a diverse array of organ system diseases.[43]

Slim Chances in "the Race of Life"

President Abraham Lincoln believed that "all men should receive a full, good, and ever increasing reward for their labors so they might have the opportunity to rise in life."[44] But he also recognized that rising entailed a "wider and fairer" world with "an unfettered start, and a fair chance in the race of life."

Today, the race of life is starting to feel rigged. Case and Deaton's identification of a "sea of despair" makes that all too apparent.[45] "There's an America for people who have gotten a college degree," Case describes, "and an America for people who have not gotten a college degree. And if you had a checklist of well-being, the people without college degrees are getting worse and worse, and people with college degrees are doing very well."[46]

The America for people without a college degree is an America of disintegrating job prospects. While it used to be possible to get a great job with benefits and to access on-the-job training with just a high school diploma, this is no longer the case. More working-age adults are shut out of the opportunity to demonstrate that they are ready and can learn.

My focus here on working-class Americans is meant neither to invoke pity nor to distinguish this enormous population of working learners as separate and different from the rest of us. Instead, by shining light on the millions of people who are being left behind today, I hope that we can see how interwoven and constrained our fates are. The future of 41 million workers is the same as the future of *us*. We are all—every single one of us—going to need to access a better-functioning learning ecosystem in the future. And we are each going to bump into the same barriers that make progress feel impossible today for a huge swath of our population.

The Future of Us

The good jobs of the future will require even more postsecondary education and training—and a broader set of skills and competencies—than the jobs of the past. Nobody really wants to go *back* to school, but more and more Americans are finding themselves in situations where they need to skill up or retool themselves to remain relevant in the labor market.

For all the talk of lifelong learning, however, educational models and funding models remain antiquated. They have not evolved to attend to adult learners. Andy Van Kleunen, CEO of the National Skills Coalition, puts it succinctly: "Many countries we compete with see continual worker retraining as part of their economic strategy. The way we've traditionally treated education in this country is the government is responsible for your education until age 18, and after that, it's more of a private matter."[47]

Most workers can already sense that things are different now—that they must somehow skill up. And this is where things get really stuck.

The situations adult learners face are radically different from those younger learners face. How is a person supposed to work full-time or stitch together multiple low-wage, part-time jobs to make ends meet, be a caregiver as well as a parent, and then, on top of all of that, figure out how to squeeze in some sort of postsecondary education or training?

The research group that I led at Strada Institute for the Future of Work captured many inspiring and heartbreaking stories of working-age adults struggling in the labor market. Through these interviews, we quickly realized that, in general, people were leveraging all kinds of hacks and side hustles to maneuver their way to something better.

One woman we spoke to explained in the calmest of voices how she, on a weekly basis, stitched together this series of activities:

> I did cut hair. People would come over and I would still do their hair at my home. But generally, my routine was—I didn't have a car at the time—I was riding a bicycle. And luckily everything in [my town] is so tiny and close by. And I would put my children on the school bus for school and ride my bike and clean houses for the doctors and the dentists down in the high-end neighborhoods and then ride my bike up to school, and I'd audio-tape my classes and ride home and meet the kids and then let them play, and cook dinner, and do all those preparatory things that you do with children. And after they were bathed and they're sitting there watching TV or relaxing before bed, I'd put on my headset, listen to my lecture again, and I'd be sewing wedding dresses at this long table that I had, and I would just be sewing dresses and listening to the lecture. And on the weekends, I was driving a taxi.

Are you exhausted yet? It's remarkable to think that these are the norms of her week. McKinsey Global Institute has shown that part-time employment "is higher than at any time since 1980," and this interviewee brings to life the notion that so many workers are pulling together multiple part-time jobs to make ends meet.[48] The resulting sensation, as another woman put it, is that "you're so raw and vulnerable in the experience. It's exhausting."

Throughout this book, you will hear more from the people who need help in launching into better opportunities. By beginning with empathy for those facing the most barriers, we can design toward those pain points and build more seamless paths—not just for one group of people, but for all of us.

Cutting into the Curb

In the early 1970s, in a makeshift gesture of defiance, Michael Pachovas and a few of his friends created sloping curb ramps in their Berkeley, California, neighborhood so that they could navigate the sidewalks in their wheelchairs. This seemingly simple act had ripple effects throughout thousands of cities beyond Berkeley.[49] In 1990, President George H. W. Bush signed into law the Americans with Disabilities Act, which prohibits any part of a built environment from discriminating against people with disabilities.[50]

When curb cuts became the new normal on streets, PolicyLink founder Andrea Glover Blackwell explains, "a magnificent and unexpected thing happened. When the wall of exclusion came down, everybody benefited—not only people in wheelchairs. Parents pushing strollers headed straight for curb cuts. So did workers pushing heavy carts, business travelers wheeling luggage, even runners and skateboarders."[51]

This is the basis of what is now known as universal design, an inclusive approach that aspires to benefit and be accessed and understood by every member of the population by promoting accessible and usable design and composition.[52] "Cut into the curb," Blackwell writes, "and we create a path forward for everyone."

In the same spirit as solving the problems posed by the sidewalk curbs, we must home in on the obstacles that more than 41 million Americans are currently encountering in the system. This approach helps sharpen our focus and target our support for those with the most challenges. "When we create the circumstances that allow those who have been left behind to participate and contribute fully—everyone wins," Blackwell says.

By cutting into the curb and focusing on those who are faltering in the cracks today, we can begin building more easily navigable pathways to meaningful careers and lives for more people. Ultimately, this isn't just about a single transition from education to work but a series of transitions over a lifetime.

No matter who we are today, or whether we already have a degree or a well-paying job, we will all need to return to education throughout our work lives to learn new skills and transition between career fields. And when we do, we'll face the same constraints on our time and resources, and the same limited options, as the millions of Americans who are being left behind today. As Dr. Martin Luther King Jr. said so eloquently, "We are caught in an inescapable network of mutuality, tied in a single garment of destiny. Whatever affects one directly, affects all indirectly."[53]

Solve for the pain points of those who are most distressed, and everyone benefits.

Part II
To a New Learning Ecosystem

4 Seamless On- and Off-Ramps

The arc of our lives is shifting away from a linear progression from education to work and retirement. A longer work life, coupled with technological advancements, will require continuous learning. More adults will face multiple career transitions, demanding the acquisition and demonstration of new skills. And that transition experience needs to feel *seamless* to learners—learners like Steve.

After determining that college was not for him when he was younger, Steve became an IT specialist, building his career while providing for his family. He is the sole breadwinner for his family—his wife, two sons, and one grandson. For the past 20 years, Steve has been crawling under desks and into attic spaces, pushing heavy carts, and responding to his colleagues' calls for assistance.

Now, at 51, Steve figures he needs to work for at least another 15 years, but he's finding the physical aspects of the job taking a toll on his body. He recognizes that it's time to make a career change. But Steve doesn't know what that path should look like, where to get started, or how to make it happen. He's considering going into teaching because it seems secure and he likes kids. Is that a good career option for him, or is it just a familiar option? Teaching will require him to go back and get his bachelor's degree, but he can't afford to stop working. Steve and his family rely on the health insurance that his job provides, and they can't afford to be without it. Without the right network of support, he doesn't know where to turn for advice.

Through stories like Steve's, we see vividly that our current systems weren't designed for adults and that the solution isn't as simple as sending Steve to community college. Most of us either know someone or can easily imagine ourselves, our friends, or relatives in the same sort of predicament.

We know from our own encounters in this web of mutuality that it's difficult to access the technologies and tools necessary to analyze our talents and gaps. It feels isolating without a trusted guide or support service to coach us on which pathways will be most effective, targeted, and affordable in helping us grow and thrive in the labor market. Oh, and how in the world are we going to pay for all of this?

Although America's higher education and workforce systems do have some solutions in place, they are fragmented bits and pieces that rarely come together in an easily navigable and seamless way. We, as the new consumers of education, will need better and more relevant information and insights, options for funding, personalized support, guidance, or connections and access to the right skills training or learning experiences that flex and meet us where we are. We'll need to spend our time and resources making measurable progress toward our next career goals rather than staying stuck, guessing at limited options, or taking unwanted detours down deadend paths. A better future learning ecosystem will show Steve and the rest of us the pathways available, help us pay for them, help us learn and get endorsed for that learning, and ultimately get us hired.

Getting Unstuck

Imagine a world in which Steve could complete a free skills assessment, created with real-time labor market intelligence, that would link his knowledge and the skills he's developed as an IT support specialist directly to jobs across various industries. Initially, he had thought teaching might be a good, steady path, given his affinity for working with children. However, the assessment reveals that Steve has transferable knowledge, skills, and abilities to transition into several different career areas—a few that he never knew existed or considered as options.

Surprisingly, teaching isn't high on that list, and Steve is intrigued by several of the options, such as client services product coordinator, IT project manager, and network systems analyst. He also learns that he has 60 percent of the skills needed to become a product manager, 30 percent of the domain knowledge to become a data science analyst, and 84 percent of the skills to be a human resources manager.

In addition to learning about his skills, Steve is directed to a website with easily comprehensible information on local and virtual training opportunities. Knowing that a geographic move is not realistic because his family is rooted in their community, Steve checks out which jobs are in demand locally and what they offer as compensation. With access to a kind of education GPS, Steve can also see others who have followed this same path and how they've fared as well as what he can expect in his own transition.

With a clearer understanding of the most viable training and employment opportunities, Steve needs to figure out how much this transition will cost and how to pay for it. Throughout the process of exploring education paths, Steve connects frequently by phone, chat, and text with a trusted advisor and also uses some tech-enabled supports. These services help Steve articulate his transition goals and decide whether he has the time and resources to take this leap based on the information available on employment opportunities, training, and funding.

He accesses information on costs, financial aid, and other financing options for additional education, and he learns about income-share agreements—financing partnerships between schools and students that allow for repayment of tuition over time based on his future income.

He likes that this option aligns the training provider's interests with his own and that he can pay for his tuition over time.

In addition to this information on funding, Steve also learns about gig work and more flexible part-time work opportunities so he can cover his cost-of-living expenses while he's learning. Equipped with this array of options, Steve can determine the right educational endeavor that will pay off and won't put his family's stability at risk. Having started programs in the past that he never completed, Steve knows that a support network will help keep him accountable in persisting in his journey. He plans to maintain regular contact with his network throughout the duration of the program.

With the help of his advisor, Steve finds the right learning experience that aligns with his chosen career path. Out of a range of offerings, including open educational resources, massive open online courses, courses through Pluralsight and Udemy, as well as a data science bootcamp, he decides to pursue a combination of locally available, face-to-face training and paid online courses. Together, these learning experiences should prepare Steve for his next opportunity in approximately six months of part-time learning.

As Steve retools himself, he has access to a peer-to-peer network for support and to on-demand tutors. The advisor who helped him begin this new pathway always stays involved with coaching and makes sure to apprise Steve of internships and apprenticeship opportunities that are aligned with his roadmap.

And as he is learning, Steve knows that he will need to translate, package, and legitimize his learning to his future employers. He will need ways of demonstrating mastery, matching his skills to the demands of the marketplace, and proving to future hiring managers that he can do the work. Steve needs a way to package his past experience and skills into a format and language that prospective employers can trust and understand.

Once equipped with his enhanced skills, Steve applies for new jobs. His future employer doesn't see a big risk in hiring him because there's clear alignment between Steve's knowledge and skills and the company's talent needs. The employer can also see that Steve has demonstrated the application of his skills through an apprenticeship program as well as the digital portfolio he has assembled.

As he transitions into his new role, Steve also understands that before he retires, he may engage in another transition just like this—or two or more. When that happens, he knows that he can leverage similar resources in his learning ecosystem to stay ahead and remain relevant in the workforce of the future.

Guiding Principles for a New Learning Ecosystem

A new learning ecosystem like the one I just described doesn't exist yet, but there's no reason why it can't. All of these bits and pieces exist in our interdependent system of learners, employers, education providers, governments, and schools. But to create a better functioning ecosystem, we will need communities and stakeholders to mobilize differently and work together toward a common vision, centered on the needs and the lived experiences of working learners, because Steve isn't the only one who will need help.

We will *all* need better ways to seek out the relevant information, funding, time, advice, support, and skills training to navigate the transitions to come. The solutions must be centered on our needs, our circumstances, and our challenges and be easy to use, affordable, and understandable.

Five Guiding Principles

For all people to thrive in the work of the future, a new learning ecosystem must incorporate these five guiding principles and be:

1. **Navigable.** People need a bird's-eye view of the current and future job market, including all of the career pathways open to them based on their interests, skills, past training, and experiences. Adults need better information on how to navigate complex systems and better assessments to help them make sense of their skills and experience and figure out how to translate and transfer their capabilities into better jobs.

2. **Supportive.** To stay focused on their education and career goals, learners need comprehensive wraparound supports, whether they are person-to-person or tech-enabled, to help them overcome hurdles and manage multiple commitments and competing priorities. Better support services will foster the success of all working learners, from the beginning of their exploration all the way through to their next job and subsequent career transitions.

3. **Targeted.** Learners need access to a precise and relevant education tailored to their needs: the right skills, the right pathways, at the right time. They also need to know that the education they choose will be worth the investment—and clearly signal value to a prospective employer. More precise or targeted learning experiences must provide not only the knowledge but also the human and technical skills, professional networks, and hands-on practice that equip learners to be ready to work.

4. Integrated. Working learners need the time, the funding, the confidence, and the resources to integrate education and training with their existing responsibilities. A new learning ecosystem will reduce education friction and make advancement achievable by offering better funding options, new opportunities to learn while earning, and, ideally, more portable benefits.

5. Transparent. The hiring process must be transparent, open, and fair—and enable job seekers to prove their competence and skills. When skills become the primary currency of the job market, employers will be able to access a more diverse pool of qualified candidates who have proved they have what it takes for the work ahead.

The connective tissue that unites these five guiding principles is a more robust data infrastructure. Data sharing is key to strengthening connections among learners, employers, learning providers, funders, and policymakers in any given community. An improved data infrastructure will not only create a shared language; it will also empower groups to move toward a common vision and integrate resources, solutions, and services to make each step along the working learner's journey a seamless and more easily navigable experience.

A new learning ecosystem will teach us the skills of tomorrow and send us smoothly on our way to rinse, wash, repeat—20 to 30 more times over a lifetime.

A Way Forward

In this second part of the book, we delve deeply into the five guiding principles of a new learning ecosystem. Each chapter is divided into three sections: "What We're Hearing," "The Predicament," and "Seeds of Innovation." We begin with the lived experiences of people, our nonconsumers, and what we're hearing from them in our interviews. Then we move into the predicaments and barriers that hold this problem in place. From that complexity, each chapter moves toward solutions, showcasing the new skills, new paradigms of teaching and learning, new business models, new pathways, new ways of hiring, and new modes of upskilling that can move us to brighter narratives for the future. By advancing from problem statements to solutions, we can adopt a more positive stance toward the future.

Over the last few decades, we have witnessed a burgeoning of new education technologies and solutions solving for one or some of the five aspects of a new learning ecosystem. LearnLaunch estimates that between 2015 and 2018, more than 240 new companies secured funding to address supply-demand mismatch issues, workplace competencies, technical skills, and informal and formal training, making up a marketplace of workforce technology in excess of $2.9 billion.[1] The ebullience of private capital spurring innovations is pushing hard against the great inertia in the system.

Over the years, I have been fortunate enough to meet hundreds of entrepreneurs, education technology providers, and organizations working in this arena—designing inventive, affordable, and accessible high-quality solutions and learning experiences for more people. These next few chapters feature some of those seeds of innovation—not as a sign of endorsement but as a way of pointing out voids in the marketplace. Many of these innovations weave together only a few of the five elements, but not all or not at scale. Moreover, some of these seeds may or may not exist in a few years or by the time you read this book. With venture capital flooding the system, there will be winners and losers among all of the entrepreneurs working in this space. The same goes for the nonprofit organizations that I highlight.

With no end in sight for the rapid changes in work ahead, we cannot continue to innovate in silos—piecing together fragmented resources or unscalable solutions that solve just one or a few aspects of the ecosystem. It will take collaboration among stakeholders in communities of all shapes and sizes to knit together the programs and solutions that can serve as engines of upward mobility for millions more working learners.

5 Navigating Our Next Job Transition

A new learning ecosystem must be **navigable**: People need a bird's-eye view of the current and future job market, including all of the career pathways open to them based on their interests, skills, past training, and experiences. Adults need better information on how to navigate complex systems and better assessments to help them make sense of their skills and experience and figure out how to translate and transfer their capabilities into better jobs.

What We're Hearing

"Where do I turn?" one interviewee asked simply.[1] "In this situation, what we need is direction. What we need is education. What we need is someone to sort of point us in the right direction, and in some cases, someone to vouch for us, you know?" Another said, "I had no GPS. I had no one to guide me."

One after another, working learners kept signaling to us in interviews that they needed direction. "There's no roadmap," one woman said. "So here we are trucking through life, and I'm feeling like I'm not good enough. I'm not making enough money. And it wasn't something my husband could fix."

Adult learners need better information to navigate complex systems—some sort of wayfinder or GPS to tell them where they are relative to where they want to go. One working learner in his 60s said: "Yeah, well, I bring the perspective of an older person, you know, trying to figure out and redefine themselves in the job market, and where do I go? I've got these sets of skills in certain areas, and it's a matter for me to define what are my likes, dislikes. I certainly know the things that I've done in the past that I didn't like. I know the things that I do like and that I have a passion for, and I sort of want to meld them together."

People are seeking direction and guidance to chart a clear path forward. The challenge, of course, is that there are no reliable or widespread assessments that can help more mature adults make sense of their years of experience as well as the kinds of skills, capabilities, and hidden assets they bring to the table.

As one person explained, "The job market we're in, it kind of puts us in the space where we feel like we have one direction. And there's no other doors, you know?" One gentleman in his 40s explained that he now feels "pigeonholed into being only in hospitality," even though he knows that it doesn't define who he truly is. Describing himself as "at that halfway point where [he]'d like to start to try other possibilities in this world," he doesn't know where to turn. Where is the GPS he needs to navigate a way forward?

For many of us, our first response might be to turn to the internet, but interviewees consistently lamented the dearth of trustworthy information on the web. One man said, "A lot of it, I've had to look on simple things like YouTube, and that simply isn't enough. You know, there really is no information on where to even get started." People need help sifting through the choices, opportunities, pitfalls, and career paths to pursue. "There's a lot of fake training that's made available online," one interviewee complained:

It happens in the bar business, too, especially with bartending school … there are people that are just designing these things and will have what seems like a very legit website and have all these fake accreditations, charge you a bunch of money, and it ends up being nothing …. I think something that we all have to be a little bit wary of is: Where is information coming from? Is it coming from a source that is trusted, or is it coming from something that you heard about from a friend? … As much as I like things like Google and because of the amount of information that's available to me … we're now in that age of information where we really have to decipher where it's coming from.

Other potential learners actually did have a general sense of direction but no understanding of how to make their aspirations become a reality. One interviewee, impressed by former President Obama's green initiatives, described his heightened interest in renewable energy: "There are so many industries that I'm interested in that I need to know how to learn more about to get into now. Green energy is … I mean, it's remarkable what Mr. Obama started, but … I still don't feel those things are accessible to someone like me. I don't even know where to begin. I'm interested in it, but I don't even know where to start." Passion or curiosity has no way of connecting to work without obvious and easily visible learning paths to get there.

Over and over again, working learners described seeking greater transparency about how to make sense of their options. They recognized clearly that education is a way to move up and ahead, but they lacked awareness of the options best suited for them.

And in a world flooded with consumer ratings, education remains one of the few bastions unscathed and unchanged by consumer perceptions. On Amazon, people can search for a laptop cable and find over 1,000 reviews for something that costs less than $10. When it comes to higher education, potential consumers of education encounter a black box.

There are scant reviews to read before someone chooses a degree, certificate, or apprenticeship program. Most learners don't know how much they'll pay prior to enrollment, let alone where previous students landed jobs after graduation. Were they able to pay off their debt? How meaningful did they find the work they were doing after they had graduated? As one interviewee said, "When you go to college, that is an investment. When you invest your money or your time into something, you expect a return on that, and not just a few pennies on the dollar of a return … you wanna have a decent return, a return on your life, your quality of life—not just a good job."

Although three-quarters or more of college presidents believe their institutions should publish information on institution-level loan debt, job placement rates, and graduate school placement rates, few, if any U.S institutions willingly offer up such information.[2] Even if some colleges do, they don't convey information in a standardized format to help families and learners make apples-to-apples comparisons of schools. For the most part, besides slick brochures, college websites, television advertisements, and highway billboards, little exists beyond College Scorecard's ratings or *U.S. News & World Report*'s often-criticized rankings to help students and families make sense of what is often one of the largest investments of their lives.

If it's hard enough to make sense of the 4,000 or so established institutions in the United States, how are learners supposed to evaluate the differences between the many alternative learning providers that have started cropping up? One interviewee mentioned that he had noticed that there was something called coding bootcamps but that most people had no way of knowing about these opportunities: "So, our whole system needs to be geared to be very, very flexible so that people are aware of opportunities. For example, one is in coding. I hear there's a huge demand for coding … . It happened to my nephew making $110,000 a year. Well, people need to be aware of these situations." The only way he found out was through a family member—someone he knew—but this critical information is not readily known by most;

or, in certain cases, interviewees told us that some of these alternatives sound way "too good to be true." How are they supposed to know what to believe?

The Predicament

The harsh effects of the future of work will distribute unevenly and unequally, varying by the kind of work, where it is taking place, and who is doing it. The people most at risk are from communities of color, especially Native American, Latino, and Black workers in lower-wage, lower-education roles that involve a lot of routine or rote work.[3] These include jobs in food preparation and serving, assembly-line production, transportation, and office and administrative support. America's heartland, in particular, will be more exposed than other regions of the country.[4]

To date, most of the burden and risk of navigating this displacement has been on us, the working learners, to somehow sort this out for ourselves. But this approach is not viable. For more learners to thrive, we need a new learning ecosystem that helps us navigate and make sense of our options and informs us that we actually do have options. In order to do that, we need better assessments, along with a guide on the side—a trusted advisor—to help make sense of our options. Better insights would help us understand where we are and where we want to go: What capabilities, skill sets, interests, and mindsets do we have? What are our gaps in relation to our goals in life?

We also need ways of translating our skills from one industry to another, recognizing that nothing is wasted—that all learning and work experience counts. There are not enough ways to measure and validate what author Peter Smith calls people's "hidden credentials," or "the actual knowledge, skills, and abilities that you have accumulated during your personal and work life ... *all* the learning you have done, throughout your life, both inside and outside of school or college."[5]

Despite the fact that a great many of our skills develop on the job and through the experience of supporting our families, there are no ways of certifying that kind of knowledge. Most employers and colleges continue to evaluate "what you know ... based on where you learned it, not how well you know it and can apply it," writes Smith.

In a 100-year work life, we'll need ways to assess all of our personal and informal learning and to transfer those assets into new or adjacent domains. How do we begin to understand that perhaps 30 percent of what we already know could be channeled into a totally different and potentially promising pathway we never even knew was within reach?

As working learners, we need guidance systems that illuminate the career pathways open to us based on our past training and experience—a panoramic or more holistic view of who we are relative to the current and future job market. Creating better navigation comes down to identifying the right human+ skills (discussed in Chapter 1) we need to develop for the future of work, along with options on the most affordable and targeted ways to fill those skills gaps to get the job we want.

Seeds of Innovation

In 1799, a French soldier fighting for Napoleon in Egypt discovered a massive piece of stone inscribed in three languages: two ancient Egyptian scripts with ancient Greek below them. The Rosetta Stone, as it was called, became the key to deciphering Egyptian hieroglyphs. This stone now has become synonymous with decoding new fields of knowledge.

In our current moment, the learner, the learning provider, and the employer are all speaking different languages. There is a profound gap in how higher education institutions and employers talk about skills. Neither side understands clearly what the other needs.

With real-time labor market data as our decoder, however, we now have access to a modern-day Rosetta Stone to connect postsecondary education and the workforce. Because we can extract the skills from job postings from businesses (demand-side data) and social profiles and resumes from people (supply-side data), we can impute more granular skills. By examining the intersection of the skills that workers are displaying in their resume and social profile data as they migrate between industries and occupations, we can then marry that data with the skills they are being hired for through employers' job postings data.[6] As a result, we can more clearly diagnose the realities of work, education, and skills requirements and how skills develop and morph across regions and industries.

Unpacking Human+ Skills

Journalism and writing careers exemplify the importance of leveraging real-time labor market information. A learner might assume that the skill that matters the most in getting a job in journalism is to be an excellent writer, but the human skill of communication is insufficient to launch a successful career. It turns out that journalism has morphed dramatically into a field that looks a whole lot more like an information technology (IT) field. (See Figure 5.1.) The data show that there has been a dramatic increase in demand for programming skills and web analytics capabilities, such as search engine optimization, JavaScript, CSS, HTML, and Google analytics.

The sizes of the circles in Figure 5.1 represent the enormity of demand for these skills in job postings data. More specifically, learners thinking about majoring in writing or journalism should understand clearly that while developing their communication skills, they must also have a strong grasp of Google analytics, search engine

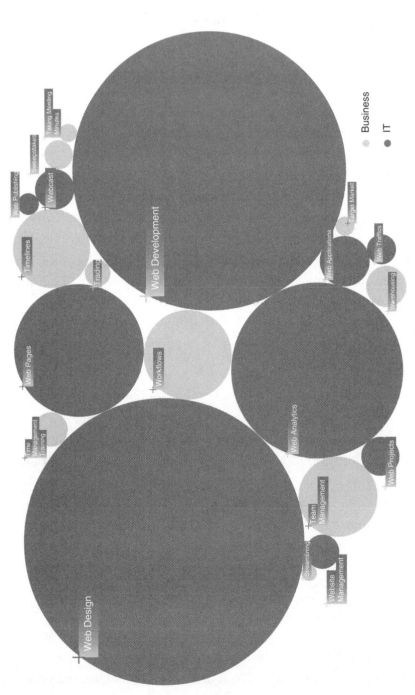

Figure 5.1 Journalism job postings increasingly require tech skills like analytics, search engine optimization, and JavaScript.

Source: Robot-Ready: Human+ Skills for the Future of Work. Emsi job posting analytics, 2018. © 2018, Strada Education Network.

optimization, and data visualization. They must also refine their communication skills to include business and marketing skills, such as brand work, content development, market research, and advertising. Those considering technical writing should be able to communicate software specifications fluently. They will also need software development and project management skills (e.g., Scrum) while having some grasp of project planning, process improvement, and program management.

Skills matter a great deal, but the right combination of human+ skills also depends greatly on the learners and the stage in which they find themselves as they seek to pivot between jobs or access new learning. For those about to make the first transition from college to work, we can see how stronger advising and career services would be needed earlier in the learning experience to guide them to the kinds of technical skills they'll need to acquire. Developing many of these human+ skills must begin early on—not right before graduation—with the active help of educators and other learning providers.

Thinking Ahead: Skills for the Next Transition and the Next One

Other more mature job seekers may need help articulating their learning goals and envisioning the possibilities. They need ways of capturing all of the knowledge and skills they have developed from experiences such as raising kids, driving a truck across the country thousands of times, or caring for a family member with Alzheimer's—and ways to frame and translate those human+ skills into the language of the labor market. They may not know how transferable their skills are from one industry to another or the gaps they need to fill. Economist James Bessen fears that, in most cases, "people are losing jobs and we're not doing a good job of getting them the skills and knowledge they need to work for the new jobs."[7]

Adults facing a layoff or life transition need to understand domain adjacencies, or how the work they're doing now can port over to what they might do in the future. They need understandable and more obvious ways to catalog their strengths, capabilities, skill sets, and experience and to get guidance on promising pathways to new careers that would meet their needs, interests, and motivations.

With clearer roadmaps and more obvious pathways to adjacent areas, working learners can understand how they transfer and apply more of their skills and strengths to new opportunities. It is why Amazon grabbed headlines in 2019 with its commitment to retrain more than 100,000 workers.[8] Not only has the company started to pay $15 per hour for warehouse workers, but it has also begun to create pathways for workers to transition to jobs as data technicians. Through a 16-week certification program, fulfillment-center employers can upskill and double their earnings along the way.[9]

Allianz, the insurance giant, is now creating "job families" out of big data to assess the skills that will be relevant in the next three years. Mike Derezin from LinkedIn explains that Allianz uses an internal assessment to understand the skills of its employees.[10] At the same time, the company curates lists of skills that align with the company's future strategy. It can then determine skills gaps that may exist or could be filled by talent within the organization.

A Skills Compass

We're going to get somewhere from here.

—Interviewee

Against this backdrop, a growing number of tech entrepreneurs and upstart innovators are working on AI-powered guidance systems to help illuminate potential pathways to greater economic opportunity. Each of these companies describes its approach slightly differently, but they are all asking the same foundational question: How do learners apply the collection of skills they have accumulated over time and find their desired career pathways?

The solutions they've developed each function as a skills compass, identifying the skills an individual or workforce already has and then pointing the way toward the right learning pathways to acquire in-demand skills of the future.

Scraping millions of pieces of data from job descriptions, government databases, and CVs, these companies are using natural language processing to make sense of structured and unstructured data. They then layer on AI-powered algorithms and neural networks to extract finer information about skills importance and volume of demand. Leveraging some sort of skills ontology or taxonomy, each platform offers both greater visibility and clear upskilling routes to better jobs.

To illustrate, Emsi, a labor market analytics firm, has created a new tool it calls SkillsMatch.[11] As people add information to the platform about their past experiences and other relevant input from their resumes, the model begins to surface competencies to help users round out their profiles.

So, as someone types in "barista," for example, the model asks, "Did you know that most people who entered barista tend to have skills in customer service, accounting, managing a team, managing a budget, etc.?" People can click on the skills that apply to them, and by the end of the process, the model identifies a handful of career pathways within reach—many of them roles they may never have envisioned for themselves. The model is able to estimate that a person is 85 percent of the way there to switch into a role in human resources and 30 percent of the way there to skill up toward being a network analyst, for example. At the same time that the tool surfaces skills gaps for people, it also connects them with learning providers and the precise courses and content to help fill those gaps.

In a similar vein, FutureFit works with the Organization for
Economic Cooperation and Development and McKinsey to help
people, companies, and governments leverage intelligence to identify
transition pathways.[12] With recommendation and matchmaking
algorithms, FutureFit has a personality profiler as well as a profile
parser to make sense of candidates' resumes and profile data and match
them to open jobs. It also layers on a skills gap analyzer and learning
recommendation app so that users can access filtered learning content
from 30,000 institutions in order to fill those skills gaps.

SkyHive calls its approach "quantum labor analysis" to encapsulate
the notion that it is analyzing a workforce at its most granular level.[13]
"People don't know their own skills, and employers don't know the
skills of their workforce. They know job descriptions and roles, and
that is it," says Sean Hinton, founder and CEO of SkyHive. "They
may not even understand how the skills required for a certain role are
changing."[14]

SkyHive's platform helps users accurately represent their current
skills as a step toward finding the right training program. Based on
users' education, job experience, or other measures, SkyHive extrap-
olates certain skills and also checks users' self-reported skill levels by
comparing them with others with similar training and experience.
Hinton describes this benchmarking step as a "social proof process."[15]
At the same time, the platform suggests specific skills that users should
consider acquiring and aggregates various educational content engines,
such as massive open online courses, employers' own training and
development content, on-demand tech skills training platforms such
as Pluralsight, and other forms of digital learning to enable that rapid
reskilling.

All of these companies are doing important work bringing to life
the concept of a skills compass. For more working learners to thrive
now and in the future, we will need even more consumer-facing
roadmaps and tools to illuminate career paths to better economic
opportunities.

Highlighting Our Most Hirable Traits

At the same time, not all navigation solutions will be tools or AI-driven platforms. The work ahead will also involve better translation and communication. For younger, first-generation college students of color looking to make the leap to their first postcollege job, Project Basta founder Sheila Sarem has created an asset-based approach to uncover the overlooked skills and talents they already possess.

Project Basta helps participants understand how to make the experiences they have count. For example, if they're aiming for a career in finance, Project Basta teaches them that a job at Target can make them just as valuable a candidate as someone who interned at an investment bank.

Job seekers learn how to convey to hiring managers why their unique experiences matter. For example, the student working 40 hours a week at Target likely learned leadership and project management skills—and that is what the hiring manager needs to hear. The key is "knowing and communicating your own value," Sarem explained. "We really have to train our young people to figure out how they own and then tell their own story."[16] When job seekers can identify and explain the relevance of what they've learned, that initial retail job becomes a stepping-stone to greater opportunity.

These same tenets hold true for older adult learners. Crossing over from an entry-level service job into a career-making corporate role can come down to speaking the same language. Using a combination of skills training and network building, Climb Hire trains people in the Bay Area for desirable, well-paying Salesforce administrator roles. Nitzan Pelman, the CEO and founder of Climb Hire, often works with her students to recast their work experience into terms that make sense to employers.

"It's been an amazing opportunity for me to learn their stories and help them translate their stories," Pelman said.[17] One of her students who was prepping for an interview told Pelman a story about coping with a delivery delay in his job at Trader Joe's. Initially, he didn't see much relevance in how he reacted to a major workforce challenge. But when Pelman repeated the student's story, using interview-friendly language to describe how he successfully managed a complex situation, the student recognized that he had demonstrated critical thinking, initiative, and quick problem solving. Just as important, he recognized how he could effectively tell that same story to a hiring manager.

In a 100-year work life, people will need more ways of translating their personal, work, and informal learning experiences into transferable skills that help them shift from one industry to another. These seeds of innovation are just the beginning.

6 Wraparound Supports

A new learning ecosystem must be **supportive**: To stay focused on their education and career goals, learners need comprehensive wraparound supports, whether they are person-to-person or tech-enabled, to help them overcome hurdles and manage multiple commitments and competing priorities. Better support services will foster the success of all working learners, from the beginning of their exploration all the way through to their next job and subsequent career transitions.

What We're Hearing

Despite an intense desire to advance, not all adult learners are ready to learn on day 1. Adults who are jobless, underemployed, or from low-income backgrounds face persistent barriers in their pursuit of education. In order to address these personal obstacles, some people need mental health counseling, financial coaching, or personalized, just-in-time guidance. At various times, they may need help navigating and accessing the wide range of services offered by local and state agencies or community-based organizations.

Intensive wraparound support systems are critical for success. Throughout our interviews, adult learners repeatedly called out the need for good guidance and trustworthy counselors to help them understand their choices and how to move forward.

Adult learners without a degree face more constraints and, in many circumstances, greater hardship than learners on campus. Having likely failed in the system before, they know they need support systems to help them assess the right paths to take; to stay accountable; and to find tutoring, transportation, childcare, and socioemotional supports.

Some supports could be enabled by technology, but for so many, human touch points are essential. As one adult learner said, "I need to be called out. I need to be spoken to. I need to be able to reach out to somebody. I have to have constant communication because that's just the way I learn. I don't know. It's different. I cannot academically do it on my own."[1]

Without the help of another human being, one learner explained how easy it was to get stuck:

> I tried to look up certain things, like I tried to look for a bunch of classes or sort of free tutorials on YouTube. I had purchased some Udemy classes, but they were from different organizations, or they're not consolidated. And I love learning, so I actually think I've probably overloaded on what I wanted to learn . . . . I'm picking a bunch of these classes that may or may not be relevant to learning Salesforce or to becoming a developer for Java . . . . When you're taking some of these [online] classes, you can get stuck. A lot of times you'll be there, you'll be stuck for a good long time before you can move on to the next concept . . . . I'm not saying that it's impossible—just that it can take a lot longer to sift through all the different solutions on YouTube or the internet.[2]

If only there was a just-in-time tutor or guide on the side to help along the way. One interviewee quietly confessed, "I personally would like just help with … maybe some counseling on how to manage time to pursue your own things that you would like to do while also trying to survive."[3]

A young mother described how she didn't realize how many things she needed, beyond childcare, until she was offered some of these wraparound supports through a program centered on adult learners. "There were so many other things I didn't realize were lacking," she said, "like the social emotional support I had of finding other parents and students that were like me." In a prior experience in a more traditional program geared toward younger, full-time learners, she noticed, "I felt super isolated, especially that math class I was taking. I didn't feel like I related to anybody—felt like I was the only parent there. I didn't want to talk about the fact that I was a parent, really .... I couldn't really engage in campus culture things. I didn't realize how much group work I was going to need to do for some of my classes, and I couldn't bring a three-year-old to a library to study with a group of other students."

Working learners need encouragement as they face the odds. Their minds are working against them as they are nagged by thoughts like these:

- "I had no hope to go back to school."
- "My biggest challenge has been overcoming those thoughts in my head that are like, 'You can't do it.' Or listening too hard to what other people say when they say that I can't do something that I know that I can."
- "Sometimes I feel like giving up, but, you know, but I don't wanna, you know ... I don't wanna do that."

Learners need coaching and advising to keep them going when life gets in the way of their pursuit of more learning. They need an extra boost of confidence to get them one step closer toward completing a program because the promise of what is next is so much more than what they have now.

Without encouragement, the system can feel rigged against them. One formerly incarcerated interviewee explained how he feels that his past mistakes continually follow him:

> I can say yes or no, you know? Have you ever been convicted? That question on an application. The box, right? So, that question comes up ... . How am I supposed to succeed? Everything keeps you stuck; you can only do so much. They want me to work doing construction, mindless work, but that's not me. I can work with my hands, but my mind is not being fed, right? My mind needs to be fed for me to feel like I'm encouraged, like I'm involved in something. I can't just show up to work and just build a building. That's just not in my DNA.

For many, it is as if the system doesn't want them to succeed. They can't get a break despite their willingness to grow and engage.

The Logistics of Getting Ahead

Compounding the challenges for working learners is the fact that nowadays, most applications are online. One interviewee explained how without a car, she was "going in and out, door to door, door to door. 'Can you hire me? Can you hire me? Can you hire me?'" And the recurring refrain was, "No, no, go home, and do it online." But she was homeless, a victim of domestic abuse, and staying in a shelter. She explained the conundrum of trying to catch another three buses to go to the library and fill out an application when she also had a child to pick up from school. And even though there was internet at the shelters, "it's not as easy sometimes because maybe 150 women were there, so they're all trying to do the same thing."

Another interviewee had an impressive background in animation and movies (even a film credit in *Apollo 13*) and suddenly found himself deeply depressed when his parents and sister all died within a short period of time. He lost his job, his car, and his home in quick succession. He was adrift, he explained:

So, at that point, I couldn't even get a job at a restaurant .... I can't even get a freaking job at a freaking restaurant. I don't have a car. There's a few restaurants around. I can't even get hired there because of my age, I don't know. Because I look a certain way, maybe I dressed ... I wasn't what they wanted. And at this time, I'm starting to look at how can I start applying for other jobs. It's so different from when I had to look for a job back in the '90s. Everything's online. How to keyword and position yourself in resumes? You're never ever getting to talk to anybody. So, I'm just lost in that aspect. I don't know how to even apply for a job anymore.

Those who are struggling to survive get further and further isolated precisely when they need the support of a community. The same person continued:

I went to a presentation at Community First Village a few months ago, and ... [the speaker] started his presentation with, "Let's just start with the definition of how people get here. And homelessness is a direct result of dramatic and catastrophic loss of family." When he said, "family," phew, man! I felt it. Of course, I get it ... if you're struggling as much as I am, then just let's hang and do this together. And we'll create stronger threads and a fiber, a network, and lift us all up. Even if it's just not sinking any further—it's just staying, but we're together—maybe lifted up a little bit.

Where are those threads, the network of wraparound supports, job seekers need at the most crucial times?

In Search of a Way Out

In interview after interview, we listened to people talk about how life got in the way, refusing to cooperate with their best intentions. And without alternative routes, many low-wage workers simply stay stuck; only 13 percent of workers without college degrees advance to a better-paying job within ten years.[4]

For some, that meant staying with a degrading job. Interviewees described negative job situations with which they were fed up.

One interviewee described her work as a form of imprisonment: "I have worked in a numerous amount of call centers, and I didn't even really like it . . . . It was more like, 'You can't get up. You have to stay there.' It was more like prison in a sense." Another interviewee described her difficult working conditions in an optometry office before pursuing her new learning pathway:

> It's just working with the people that are not great communicators—kind of a negative environment. There's only smiles and happiness and respect when there are patients around. . . . I also dealt with a little bit of racism there which was very hurtful, and I dealt with that for almost six months . . . . I spoke with [the HR rep] every time that I had an issue, hoping that it would get better, and [it] actually got worse . . . . So, at that point I knew that nothing would change [there]. And then speaking with coworkers, learning that it's always been that way, always been kind of a . . . negative environment. People would have to walk on eggshells around certain people, and you have to deal with a lot of crap.[5]

The more they were mistreated, the greater their desire was to get training for jobs where they would be appreciated and feel valued. One participant told us that he had been working as a salesclerk before starting a data science bootcamp: "I was working at a shoe store, and I was the manager there, but I was being lied to. They were saying that they were going to open a new store. They're going to open some new store, then give me my own store. And they ended up closing every store in the U.S. So, it was crazy. After I realized they lied to me, I realized I could do so much better . . . . I just wanted more."[6] He knew that he needed to find a new path. The lie from the management team was the last in a long line of bad experiences. He described a voice inside him that nudged, "I am better than my current situation. I know it."

In the midst of hardship and isolation, adults need the right human and tech-enabled supports, so they can stop floundering and make progress in their lives. One interviewee explained the dramatic shift in outcomes with a bit of help: "I spent ten years trying to find out what my passion was, what direction to take. And I feel like in one year, I had more opportunities and more shifts in my outcome than the other nine. And that was because I had help."

The Predicament

The new consumers of education are stuck. They are living in poverty, surviving on food stamps, and have public health insurance plans like Medicaid.[7] Working-class adults often lack basic economic necessities, such as health insurance, transportation, computers, smartphones, and internet access, which only exacerbates the challenge to make forward progress in their lives. Without easy access to the internet, millions are not able to tap into job boards to seek work, websites to apply for work, or email to contact potential employers. Lack of adequate transportation limits their ability to work in areas beyond a comfortable radius from their homes.

They do not have access to reliable sources of good information, good data, and good navigation or advice on how to manage their life and career transitions. Most working learners are asked to stack training on top of all of the other demands in their lives, from working full-time jobs (or multiple part-time ones) to caring for families and the elderly.

Adults routinely drop out of college because these kinds of circumstances and personal challenges undercut their progress in moving from education to employment. As we consider building blocks for the future, perhaps the most critical element to get right will be a deliberate focus on 360-degree support services. Wraparound supports are essential in empowering people to overcome the obstacles in their personal and work lives so they may make room for learning and new training.

Seeds of Innovation

In order to get a fair shot at the opportunities available, learners need resources and services that will help them tackle the barriers that have dogged them in the past and prevented them from acquiring the skills they need to get and keep a job that pays well. Wraparound supports are crucial in promoting persistence and completion of education and training programs. These supports include counseling, mental health services, financial advice, and even financial assistance for housing costs and transportation. Sometimes barriers to work are smaller than one would imagine—a participant might need new truck tires, steel-toed boots, or a set of knives for culinary school.

It sounds simple, but one of the most revolutionary things that City University of New York did in its Accelerated Study in Associate Programs initiative was to provide learners with a free unlimited MetroCard to get to and from school and work on the subway or bus. This perk solved a major pain point for potential learners, as did other program offerings, including access to advisors and free textbooks.

Other schools have begun building food pantries and clothing closets to attend to the day-to-day needs of their learners with fewer resources. Some schools have started to keep the campus open during breaks for students who cannot afford to go home during the holidays.

Los Angeles Valley College offers a Family Resource Center with a lactation room with a refrigerator designated for breast milk and a full kitchen for learners to bring their lunches. Learners are offered school supplies, free baby clothes and supplies, playgroups for kids, and access to a child development specialist as well as a licensed marriage and family therapist. These small shifts and adjustments are not rocket science but good common sense.

Michael Sorrell, the president of Paul Quinn College, an urban work college in South Dallas, Texas, is thinking about all aspects of support. He has raised money from philanthropies to pay for the smallest items, such as eyeglasses for learners who can't afford them. Every one of his 280 students has a job at the college, and Sorrell has even negotiated with UT-Southwestern to provide free mental health services to his learner population who, in Sorrell's words, "have been forced to endure trauma growing up that I can't begin to describe."[8]

Getting Ready to Learn

Training and upskilling alone are often not enough for adult learners. Programs must provide resources to address the conditions of their participants' lives head-on. LaunchCode, a coding apprenticeship, has partnerships with community agencies to provide public transportation and parking, legal services, food stamps, health care, and employment assistance.

JobTrain, a Silicon Valley–based workforce organization, offers on-site services to help participants gain access to legal advice, affordable childcare, and referrals. This approach is especially critical for highly marginalized populations, such as the formerly incarcerated, a core population of the 190,000 people JobTrain has already educated. These sorts of intensive services allow learners to address more personal issues before entering career-specific training. As CEO Barrie Hathaway explains, "If we can stabilize somebody prior to and during the training, they're going to persist and complete the training program."[9]

STRIVE, which started in New York City and now operates in 20 cities nationwide, assigns case managers to all learners. The case managers help with issues such as mental health, financial stability, and challenging family situations. "We have a good support team behind us," one learner said. "They know life happens behind the scenes, outside of class, or before the class. They always get in touch with us. There's just a strong support network at this program. That's why I think it's very successful." These crucial services and supports help coordinate family life, so that personal challenges are less likely to undercut progress toward and in employment.

A Guide on the Side

Human touch points are critical. One woman explained the profound effect of human contact: "They start to feel like a mentor, and you feel accountable also. You know you want to heal. I believe that it's about you. It's about your personal, intimate self-reflection that you want to heal your past—that you want to overcome anything, that you need to overcome in order to succeed."

Another interviewee recounted spending a few weeks working with a STRIVE counselor who explained to him, "'You'll get a MetroCard every day to travel to and from class. It's going to take this long,' you know. And I'm like, 'That doesn't make any sense.' But she was like, 'No, they'll get you ready for interviews, how to talk to people, how to conduct yourself in interviews,' stuff like that. And when I went to STRIVE, it was everything she told me and then some, which is why I could not forget her."[10] The team at STRIVE, and that counselor in particular, went out of their way to show that they cared about this man and valued his development as a learner and worker. And in his classes, his instructor spoke directly to his sense of self-worth. He remembers his teacher advising him: "Don't let your jobs lowball you. Don't let them tell you this is what they're going to be paying if you know that you deserve more." This particular learner's instructor consistently encouraged him and boosted the group's self-esteem, so they would know that they were worth the careers and the pay that they were pursuing.

One learner from Jewish Vocational Service underscored the abiding, long-term commitment of the counselors: "Their goal for us is to get a career job and to grow. It's not just a regular program where you just go and get your certificate, that's it, or do your internship, then basically you're on your own after that. They really want you to work hard, and then network, and then get a long-term career."

Scaffolded with robust wraparound services, learners develop grit and persistence as well as strategies to overcome future obstacles in both their personal lives and their work lives. Learners are taught not only the skills for their chosen job path but also the life skills that are critical to long-term career success and upward mobility.

A Different Kind of College for Adults. College Unbound is located in Providence, Rhode Island, and is a degree-completion college tailored specifically for adult learners. The school started off as an idea in 2009 with ten learners gathered in a makeshift classroom; it has since expanded to serve over 200 learners. Now the 13th college in Rhode Island, College Unbound is covered by federal student aid.

The average age of its students is 38. Most are female and minorities, and 80 percent work full time. More than 60 percent have an annual income that ranges between $25,000 and $45,000. Before finding College Unbound, they had given up hope of earning a degree because they could not figure out how to fit school into their daily lives.

This is not your typical college. President Dennis Littky, also the cofounder of The Met School and Big Picture Learning, and cofounding provost Adam Bush detail the ways in which College Unbound has been redesigned from the bottom up. "We're taking seriously the trauma of past educational institutions," Bush explains, "and take that responsibility to create a different kind of college that doesn't just inherit the back room and the structures of college as it was but tries to reimagine what college should be."[11]

Littky underscores the importance of overhauling the traditional college experience for adult learners because "their past experience is they've been failures. And the system has defined them as a failure." Therefore, in this new environment, all of the things that had previously been positioned as barriers in their lives, such as work, commutes, and kids—all of the things that pull them away from being a good student—are reframed as "the pieces that make them more engaged in the world around them, more critical citizens, and able to really imagine how to collaboratively do work in new ways," Bush explains. "So, the pieces that other colleges or other workplaces or other things might see as deficits, we see as assets and important parts of this curriculum."

The defining characteristic of this school is its robust 360-degree wraparound services. Classes meet one night a week in the same buildings as the Met School, an innovative daytime high school that Littky also cofounded as the flagship school of Big Picture Learning, a network of more than 100 schools. College Unbound is a tidy brick campus, set in the heart of the most difficult neighborhood in South Providence (there are also satellite campuses in Newport and Middletown, and the program is also embedded in businesses and nonprofits in the area). It offers dinner and babysitting, which enables many of these low-income learners to be present and engage actively.

In an effort to build meaningful relationships, learners break bread together before diving into the class materials. "We have a chance for people to be a part of one another's lives," Bush says. And these relationships build an important sense of community and support for all of the challenges that come with integrating learning into their busy routines.

The community that College Unbound fosters empowers its learners to solve their way out of the challenges that life brings—together. One woman in the program had gotten in a car accident and lost her car. She and her classmates held a bake sale that made $200 in half an hour, so she could buy a used car and get back to work.

Another woman was suffering from domestic abuse. She and her boyfriend were living out of a car, and Littky recounts, "he took her computer because he didn't want her to go to college, because then she'd leave him, which is probably right—smart boy. And so, we were doing work with her to try to protect her—get her to a safe house. And she said, 'Never before have I ever had this much support in my life.'"

By spending an hour with her to get her the services she needed, the team at College Unbound was able to remove her from an extremely difficult situation.

Participants also get access to a financial aid counselor, whom Littky describes as someone who goes above and beyond what a person might find in a traditional school. He's "talking to them, building a relationship with them, going down to the IRS with them, delivering a check to their house, helping them get off default."

All of these interventions and wraparound supports are making a difference. The school has an 80 percent completion rate with 87 percent employed full-time and 20 percent going on to graduate school. Littky's plan is to leverage Big Picture Learning's existing network of 150 schools to scale this program around the country.

Networking and Social Capital

Another crucial element of wraparound supports is the development of social capital. Julia Freeland Fisher, the author of *Who You Know*, explains that "social capital is an asset, just like financial—or even human capital. It is made up of your 'network,' or the constellation of relationships that you use to get things done."[12]

People used to view social capital as largely fixed or inherited. Social networks appeared to be largely based on the networks of parents who, in turn, passed their networks on to their children. But a growing body of research suggests that social capital is learnable and that those who lack social capital can be taught how to build it.

Building and diversifying access to social capital has become a cornerstone of many newer programs. Nitzan Pelman started Climb Hire to help learners build and grow their own social capital. After learning from research that people are nine times more likely to get a job through a referral, Pelman began shadowing other leaders and entrepreneurs who are working on issues of social capital.[13]

She modeled her company on Kalani Leifer's program called COOP, in New York, which creates cohorts of underemployed graduates from City University of New York, San Francisco State, and other urban public colleges, and skills them up to work in digital marketing roles. COOP meets nightly from 6 to 9 pm—in-person always. At the end of the training, all participants get a job, but their work doesn't stop there.

The job of a COOP graduate is to pull in others. Once inside a company, they seek out ways to make referrals and suggest other participants for new opportunities through a peer network. They also go back and become the teachers who train the next batch of students. Learners give back both by helping others get jobs and by being the teachers. Five years in and with 1,000 alumni, the results are impressive: 80 percent of COOP participants land first-time digital marketing jobs—mostly through referrals from one another.

Inspired by the core tenets of COOP, Climb Hire focuses on a different job—becoming a Salesforce administrator—and leverages online education for more of a hybrid learning experience. The typical Climber holds multiple minimum-wage jobs, does not have a college degree, and takes classes on the weekends or evenings. Participants engage in 100 hours of online Salesforce training plus 100 hours in-person. Fifty hours are for professional skills training as well as community and social-capital building; the other 50 hours are for more Salesforce training—done face-to-face.

Climb Hire provides a weekly stipend during the program. After graduating and securing a full-time job that pays at least $45,000 annually, Climbers pay it forward to support future classes. Using a cooperative business model, alumni become part of a staffing agency. As they refer one another into roles and job opportunities, they share in the future profits generated from finders' fees from employers.

Pelman's goal is to create a self-sustaining business model in which students "are incentivized to care about social capital financially and communally."[14]

Virtual Communities. The development of social capital and broader networks doesn't always need to happen in person. Jobcase is a platform for the future of work that provides working people with the tools and resources to take control of their own careers. CEO Fred Goff explains that people, especially those who do not have advanced skills or degrees and are seeking to earn a living wage, have not been prepared for this new world of work. "They were not trained to navigate their own careers."[15]

Launched in 2015, Jobcase consists of profiles, connectors, and community. The profiles are where people keep their resumes, reviews, praise, and recommendations. The idea is that a Dunkin' employee with great reviews from her manager has a leg up when Starbucks is looking for new talent. When people control their own profiles, Goff explains, "you don't have to constantly re-prove yourself on the same things."

Connectors include job boards such as Indeed and CareerBuilder as well as reviews from GlassDoor; the connectors make it easy for people to access everything in one spot while also enabling employers to use Jobcase to recruit talent, as Home Depot has done.

And the community section of Jobcase is for empathy building and emotional support. This part of the site is what Goff calls the "secret sauce." Modeled on Quora and Reddit, the community section is where Jobcasers come to get answers about their work lives, such as wage issues and the anxiety that comes with not hearing back from companies or experiencing rejection after rejection.

With the help of strangers, people find comfort, inspiration, and practical support. "In a world where social media can seem toxic," one

Jobcase visitor said, "people here are remarkably kind to one another, posting their successes or asking for prayers before an interview."[16] The community has grown to 109 million users—29 million are active monthly users—making this the fourth largest online career platform in the United States, or a "killer app."[17]

One of the most fascinating developments of this support system is that because of its popularity and community-building capabilities, Jobcase is trying to figure out how to create a modern union to harness the power of workers. Goff explained that a group of Uber drivers in Houston had started a group on Jobcase to discuss tactical issues, such as the best times to drive or how to get into the UberEats program. As gig workers, it's nearly impossible for Uber drivers to know one another. Jobcase gives them that sense of community.

As it happened, one man who had been driving for Uber full-time was suddenly kicked off the app and told his picture was too old. He tried to connect with Uber, but no one was responding. Meanwhile, he lost all of his income over an eight-day period and was worried about making rent. Goff forwarded the conversation to a representative at Uber Houston and wrote, "Four hundred of your drivers are watching the conversation." Almost immediately, the driver was reinstated and paid eight times his daily earnings to make him whole. Goff chalks this up to the power of the community and how it can be harnessed.

For all of the ways in which technology can paradoxically make us feel hyperconnected and yet strangely alone, Jobcase is a great instantiation of the effort to forge more authentic and empathetic encounters and bonds between those seeking support and solidarity. In the learning ecosystem of the future, there will need to be more ways for people to forge stronger social ties and build connected communities.

Career Entry and Advancement Supports

In the limbo of navigating a job transition, we might think that the hardest part is landing a good job. Indeed, when a working learner is stuck in a bad job, access to a better opportunity seems like the Holy

Grail. But wraparound supports can't stop at job attainment, because once on the job, new hires can find it difficult to navigate their new work environment.

This is true for any new hire, but it is especially true for adults who have had limited employment experience and come from more disadvantaged backgrounds. Even being equipped with all of the right technical skills doesn't ensure success. Given their past work and social experiences, new hires are more at risk of leaving a job when they have a setback. They may also succeed in their first position but find themselves stuck and unable to advance to more secure and better-paid career opportunities.

There is growing evidence that postplacement supports can play a major role in helping new hires from the most vulnerable learner populations acclimate to workplace culture.[18] Continued wraparound services can empower new hires to overcome early challenges and plan for their next steps within the firm or organization. Patrick Clancy of Philadelphia Works believes that "once employees successfully get to at least six months, they can be successful in both the industry and in the role."[19] Philadelphia Works therefore assigns a case manager to new hires for six months and tracks job retention six and 12 months out postemployment.

But, according to JobTrain's CEO Hathaway, it is very difficult for many organizations to staff and pay for postplacement support for learners after they complete the program. "That's where the real gold rings are, at this point," Hathaway says. "We've got the model down in terms of high-result career education training and service provision. We've got that. It works really well. So, our leading edge is employer relations and long-term career advancement strategies."[20]

Some employers understand and are concerned about the challenge of churn among new hires, especially working-class adults. For the employers we interviewed, a new hire's longevity in a job is a core measure of value. Jennifer Stredler, vice president for workforce at Salesforce.org, explains: "No employee is perfect; even with our best interns, they're going to have times when they struggle. There are times when small challenges or barriers may create doubt and uncertainty, causing them to question whether they belong. It's very high stakes."[21]

Employers bear some of the burden of postplacement support of new hires—not just by managing but also by guiding their new employees. Robert Kress, managing director for security at Accenture, who helped grow the company's relationship with i.c.stars, a technology training program for low-income learners, describes this onus on the employer partner: "It is more challenging for some of the i.c.stars and similar folks who join us because they often need a little more mentoring or coaching and guidance just because of their backgrounds. They're typically not from families with business experience or don't have knowledge of what the expectations are to work in a Fortune 500 company, and it's different. It's just a different culture—a different set of expectations."[22] Employers frequently have unspoken expectations and hierarchies on the job that aren't clear to a new hire, particularly to someone with a limited work history. But they can minimize the friction by providing mentors and helping trainees get acclimated to a new environment and culture and the tacit expectations of their workplace.

Another barrier is that "managers are busy and strapped for time," explains Stredler. "Some also don't recognize the need for coaching and support. They say, 'Oh, I've managed people before. I don't need training.' But we know that training for managers of interns from our programs is critical to their collective success."[23]

Employers cannot expect to be passive recipients of new talent streams. They need to give new hires substantive projects and constructive coaching and feedback. They must be strong and active partners, so that new hires can acclimate to the work environment, weather initial difficulties, and understand what it will take to succeed and advance in the job. Continuous support can ultimately reduce churn, increase return on investment, and have significant long-term benefits for new workers as they prepare for success in the new economy.

7 Targeted Education

A new learning ecosystem must be **targeted.** Learners need access to a precise and relevant education tailored to their needs: the right skills, the right pathways, at the right time. They also need to know that the education they choose will be worth the investment—and clearly signal value to a prospective employer. More precise or targeted learning experiences must provide not only the knowledge but also the human and technical skills, professional networks, and hands-on practice that equip learners to be ready to work.

What We're Hearing

Jaylen is a machinist who works for an aeronautical company in Wichita.[1] He never got a degree, but his wages have allowed for a good life in the area: a family, a modest house, and a reasonably comfortable lifestyle. He's been in the labor market for 15 years and makes $40,000 annually, but his job is starting to look very different due to the forces of automation on his manufacturing role.

His boss sees potential in him and has conveyed to Jaylen that she'd love to start putting his deep knowledge of machining principles to work in an oversight capacity. There's just one problem—the new role requires a more sophisticated set of skills than Jaylen currently possesses. While his boss could hire a college graduate in engineering, she would prefer to promote Jaylen from within, especially since people like him with foundational production skills are key to the company's major transition to lean manufacturing. The company has therefore offered to pay for him to further his education.

Getting a degree at this point in his life would be a big lift, and Jaylen is overwhelmed by the idea of four years of night school. Such a long-term commitment would be difficult to square with his family life, especially for a father like him who makes a point of being at all of his kids' soccer games. What his employer views as a generous opportunity feels like a near-impossible feat.

Many adults like Jaylen know they need more training. Pew research reveals that the vast majority (87 percent) of adults in the workforce today recognize that they need to develop new skills.[2] One interviewee repeated, "I need training, I know. Definitely. I definitely know I need that."[3]

Adult learners already sense that they need something extra. A Strada-Gallup survey asked adults whether they felt like they needed additional education to advance their careers. Not surprisingly, the largest number of yeses came from those with less than a high school education.

Even more salient, however, were the responses from folks who had initially pursued career or technical education (CTE) earlier on in their lives. They were the second largest group to say yes to this question. This was the same group that had ranked their education most favorably when compared to people with a high school degree only, as well as associate, bachelor's, or graduate degree holders. CTE learners consistently viewed their education as the most valuable and relevant to their careers—more than any other contingent surveyed.

At the same time, however, they also saw the greatest need for more education: 52.5 percent acknowledged they needed more postsecondary education to advance, compared to 39 percent of those with bachelor's degrees.[4]

But which is the right training? In search of the right next thing, many adults automatically assume they need a degree. In Jaylen's case, it was the next natural step.

The Degree as the Golden Ticket

Working learners see the clear value of degrees because they've witnessed employers use degrees as proxies for talent and capabilities. More job postings than ever list a degree as a requirement—even for roles that never previously required one. Without "the piece of paper" or "the ticket," as many interviewees described it, they're stuck, unable to communicate the skills and experience they've accumulated over a lifetime of work.

A college degree is the main sorting mechanism, the first step in getting into the "yes" pile. One man explained, "I was laid off. And for the first time, the relevance of not having a degree became manifest, because even though I had years upon years—over 20 years of experience doing all these different things—the first question they were asking is 'So where did you go to school?' ... They just look at 'Has he gone to school? No.' So then you go into that pile."

From one job posting to another, working learners have become acutely aware of what they lack. One person said, "I started to find myself professionally stagnant ... and there's only so many rooms you can get in without the paper. And so I thought, 'Well, I got to get the paper.'"

Another interviewee likened a degree to a driver's license. As he shopped the classified section of the newspaper, he realized, "Gee, a bachelor's degree is like having a driver's license. That's kind of the minimum—the benchmark minimum." One musician we spoke to, who left a prestigious degree program before graduating, said that he felt automatically barred from applying to most jobs. He needed "that paper," he said, "that shows what you know."

In the search for a new job or a way to advance, a formal degree can serve as job-market shorthand validating years of experience. One woman explained that she knew she wanted to pursue a career that aligned with her volunteer work, but she also recognized that she "didn't have the tools to be able to do that, or certainly tools that might be formally recognized" to get paid to work in community advocacy and engagement. She said, "I feel like I could learn to do most jobs . . . but I understand the reality of the job market is you have to come in saying, 'I already know how to do this.' No one's going to give you six months to figure out how to do a job." Going back to school becomes a way for working learners to make their skill set "official" in the eyes of employers.

A college degree sends a specific signal. One young woman said, "Being an educator, a museum educator, people eventually want you to have some kind of degree, even if that's not where you got most of your learning from. It represents something to people." The signal has power.

It even provides some with a second chance in life. One formerly incarcerated adult said, "I knew that in order to make a livable wage at the time—I think they were paying me like a little over minimum wage, which you know, you can't live on if you wanted to—I knew that I needed more. I needed to put something in front of my name or behind my name to, one, separate myself from being a criminal and also to make me legitimate in some ways."

Not Designed for Working Learners

Degree programs seem like the obvious path for so many because they serve as an endorsement, a way to check a box and be legitimized and validated. In our interviews, adult learners affirm the signaling power of a college degree and how essential it is in opening doors. Attaining a degree, therefore, seems like an obvious path forward for many.

Unfortunately, however, the current education system wasn't designed to serve working learners, the new consumers of education. Universities have not broadened their view of whom to serve and how differently they must serve learners at various stages of their lives. "Life just happens," one interviewee said. "I think I almost lost my house in foreclosure while I was in college … so I was fighting for my property going through a Chapter 13 foreclosure, still working a full-time job, part-time job, still in school full-time, had another child, my third child."

Adults are inundated with responsibilities, and they are struggling to stay afloat. "I really needed to work full-time while continuing and pursuing an education, and the traditional college setting really isn't conducive to that," explained one woman. "So, one class on a Saturday morning or one class one night a week was all I could do when you added in full-time employment and responsibilities at home."

Life gets in the way was the recurring refrain. One woman described the challenges of juggling so much at once:

> After high school, I did try to continue my education, going to City College, and it just didn't work for me at the time. I decided to get into the working field, and … I'm like, okay, I'm doing security. This is not where I see myself in ten years. [That] kind of opened my mind back to going to school. I actually attended Chico State in the fall of 2008, and I was there for … a little over a year. And then … I ended up becoming pregnant while I was in Chico State, and that's when I withdrew … and moved back to San Francisco. After that, I was basically just holding down a job and was a single parent raising my son, and I'm just trying to find my way through life.[5]

Traditional postsecondary learning experiences don't do a great job of meeting learners where they are. Another woman described the lengths she would go to in order to squeeze in education into her week: "I lived across the street from campus, so I would go home to bring [my baby] the bottles that I had pumped in between classes because I would stack my classes to be all in one day, so that way, I could work the other days. Sometimes I would be on campus from 8:00 am till 10:00 pm at night. I would just have classes all day long."[6]

College lacks the flexibility and convenience for people who can't enroll even as part-time students because often they are working multiple jobs to sustain their families. One man explained that he understood that a degree could open doors for him. It was "something I already knew," he said. "But I couldn't go back to the traditional setting of college. I couldn't go at that time—like 25, 26, 27, 28—I couldn't go back and sit down in a classroom with 17-, 18-, 19-year-olds. It just didn't work for me—that traditional type of classroom setting."

That sentiment of age mismatch was echoed frequently. "I think as an adult learner you need other adults in the room who get you," a woman said. "Otherwise, if I was in a classroom full of 21-year-olds, I wouldn't still be there …. It helps you stay going. Everyone else has kids or a partner or somebody at home, and a job and a thing to do …. And you need that to feel validated in your insanity as an adult."

Another woman humorously described the college-going experience as otherworldly: "When I went to orientation, it was crazy. It was overwhelming. I saw all these young people sitting next to me and I was like, 'I do not belong here. What am I doing?' These are kids that are coming out of high school, and I can be their mother! That's what I'm going to be in the classroom and I really don't want to be that." The traditional setting can leave more mature learners feeling out of place—as if they don't belong.

The Need for Personalized Learning

In the end, the return to education can feel demoralizing. One interviewee delved into the off-putting nature of introductory classes:

"They put me in very remedial classes—like your starter kit .... So it wasn't that boost of confidence that I needed." And in some cases, the system demands a certain scaffolding of remedial courses that one interviewee described as taking "a bunch of classes that don't even count."

The educational experience can feel duplicative—like a waste of time and money. One woman said that she wished she could have gotten credit for what she already knew, "rather than wasting [her] time and money, wrapping it up in a neat bow and putting it on paper." She wished she could prove that "I already have this knowledge without having to do it for eight to ten weeks that costs me $4,000 every ten weeks." But people do it because they aren't aware of any other options.

Our interviewees kept telling us that they needed an educational pathway that offered the right skills at the right time that could flex with them as they desperately sought to earn a living wage. One adult learner at a for-profit university put it this way:

> And you hear so many awful things about these for-profit schools, but it was the only way I would have ever been able to succeed. As much as my parents helped and supported me, there's no way I could have been full-time on campus, going to classes day in, day out, working full-time, taking care of two kids, balancing life's speed bumps and everything else. It just … it would have been impossible. I mean, it's taken me almost 20 years. It probably could have taken me easily 50 to do it any other way.

Twenty years to complete a degree? The interviewee described the learning experience as a gift, but, sadly, even some of the most innovative online or asynchronous programs are too rigid in structure for working learners. Most can't fathom how they might square degree attainment—its duration and lack of flexibility—with work, children, and financial woes.

The Predicament

The signaling power of a degree has no equal in the labor market. But getting a two- or a four-year degree is not the only path to getting ahead. Research led by Mark Schneider while he was at American Institutes for Research shows that in certain cases, a certificate can pay off with middle-class earnings—and sometimes can even exceed the earnings of graduates with bachelor's degrees in those same fields.[7]

In states such as Colorado, Texas, and Virginia, students with associate degrees and certificates in certain fields, such as allied health diagnostic, intervention, and treatment professions, criminal justice and corrections, and fire protection—credentials that help students learn how to fix things or fix people—have high earnings. Schneider and his team tracked seven different states longitudinally to reveal that those earnings premiums were true not just for the first year out of school but also five and ten years out of these programs.

The challenge is that most learners don't even know about these programs. Jaylen's predicament earlier in the chapter shows his lack of awareness of options for more precise skills-building pathways that don't involve four years of night school. In most cases, people assume that a degree is the surest path to success and haven't heard about promising alternative pathways with strong outcomes outside of traditional higher education or don't know which ones to trust.

At the same time, it's not as if there is a vast array of these more targeted educational pathways for working learners to update and upgrade their skills without duplicating ones they have already mastered. We need more tailored pathways that are modular in nature with just-in-time training for not only technical skills but also human skills development. More college or more graduate school is not the answer here, for even our most prestigious schools are not necessarily setting learners up for success in the labor market.

Far Transfer

In an infamous vignette, a film crew captured newly minted college graduates from Harvard's and MIT's engineering programs in their caps and gowns. The crew handed each of them, one by one, a bulb with a battery and a wire. They were asked to light the bulb. Almost all of the engineering grads failed to perform this simple task.[8]

"Probably the single biggest challenge that you see in the science of learning is a problem of transfer," says Stephen Kosslyn, former Dean of the Faculty of Arts and Sciences at Harvard. "By which I mean you learn something in one context, typically in a classroom, and then you fail to use it when it's appropriate in different contexts."[9]

This idea of transfer motivated author David Epstein to write an entire book on *range*, the concept of deep analogical thinking, or "the practice of recognizing conceptual similarities in multiple domains or scenarios that may seem to have little in common on the surface."[10] Those deep connections enable the deepest learning. "When a knowledge structure is so flexible that it can be applied effectively even in new domains or extremely novel situations, it is called 'far transfer,'" Epstein writes.

Transfer is critical in an age when content is no longer king. Rather than memorize content, learners must build habits of mind that stretch across disciplines and transfer from one context to another.

Academic Silos

As much as colleges and universities believe that they are preparing students with range, the underlying structures of our postsecondary system betray how stovepiped these efforts are. For hundreds of years, institutions of higher education have artificially separated subjects from one another.

Salman Khan, the founder of Khan Academy, criticizes the foundational structure of a college—departments—as "ghettoizing" learning (his words) in his book *The One World Schoolhouse*:

> Genetics is taught in biology while probability is taught in math, even though one is really an application of the other. Physics is a separate class from algebra and calculus despite its being a direct application of them. Chemistry is partitioned off from physics even though they study many of the same phenomena at different levels. All of these divisions limit understanding and suggest a false picture of how the universe actually works.[11]

Khan blames the "balkanizing habits of our current system" for denying students "the benefit—the physiological benefit—of recognizing connections."

In the artificial siloing of subjects, learners lose out on connecting ideas across multiple disciplines. Learners are brought up thinking that problems are always domain-specific—that we learn how to solve this kind of equation as a math problem or a biology problem or an economics problem divorced from its historical context and its connections to anthropology, policy, or literature.

The result is "narrow critical competence," explains James Flynn, a professor at University of Otago in New Zealand. Flynn told Epstein: "Even the best universities aren't developing critical intelligence. They aren't giving students the tools to analyze the modern world, except in their area of specialization. Their education is too narrow."[12]

Lack of Range

To illustrate this overly specialized model of education, in *Range*, Epstein highlights the research of Dedre Gentner, creator of the Ambiguous Sorting Task. Participants review 25 cards that connect on two levels. This problem set tests whether people can move beyond the simple disciplinary connections (economics, biology, etc.) to deeper structural relationships.

Gentner tested students at Northwestern University and found that most majors could connect these cards on a domain level; however, few could go deeper and group them by their causal structures. Only one group excelled at this activity—the students from Northwestern's Integrated Science Program, a mix of biology, chemistry, physics, and math, all combined into one major.

But programs like the Integrated Science Program, which empower learners to grasp connections across disciplines, are often rarities on campus, even unwelcome. Interdisciplinarity often turns into more of a buzzword rather than real practice in postsecondary education. Indeed, Olin College of Engineering, which doesn't have any academic departments, stands out as a real anomaly in higher education.

Seeds of Innovation: Right Skills, Right Path, Right Time

If predictions about the future of work are borne out, the world will need more solvers, or people who know how to think on their toes and exercise judgment in the most ambiguous of situations. Employers are and will continue to seek out candidates with skills in systems thinking and communication, who demonstrate initiative and mental dexterity as well as emotional intelligence. Far transfer and analogical thinking will be critical for the complex problems that will accompany the work of the future.

Artificial intelligence and neural networks perform at high levels when their structures are stable and narrow. But the problems of the future will be broad and wicked. Working learners will therefore need the human+ skills to adapt to any conceivable situation. Workers who can creatively adapt and learn how to solve new problems in the market will thrive.

But problem solving requires practice. It is not an innate human skill. We will need more targeted education available throughout our longer work lives to build and strengthen this combination of technical and social and analytical skills.

The Case for Problem-Based Learning

Talk to me ... and I will forget
Show me ... and I will remember
Involve me ... and I will understand
Step back ... and I will act

—Confucius

In order to cultivate more nimble agents of the future and prepare them for the new, cross-functional jobs of tomorrow, we need to develop 21st-century learning pathways that move away from memorization and standardized testing to problem-based inquiry that fosters creativity, resilience, and innovation. We know that whenever humans solve any problem in the world, the solution is and will be, by nature, transdisciplinary. Teaching and learning, therefore, must be problem based.

"Problem-based learning" and "project-based learning" are terms that have become interchangeable over time. Both are methods in which students engage in meaningful, real-world problem solving—sometimes by actively engaging in already defined, discrete projects, and other times, through more open-ended problems that students must identify and structure themselves. I'll use "problem-based learning" throughout this section both for the sake of simplicity and also to signal the desire to make this learning format more widespread—moving beyond the confines of a course or project.

Problem-based learning involves hands-on experimentation, where learners engage in a "productive struggle"[13] and, in the midst of that struggle, persist and learn—just in time—specific disciplinary concepts. In certain cases, learners make meaning of theories through a specific context or experience and convert those theories into practical applications. In the act of trying to survey land, as an example, it suddenly becomes clear why the concepts of sine, cosine, and tangent are important to master. Or learners develop prototypes, models, or artifacts for experimentation, testing, and improvement. Rather than learning passively about the physics and physical workings of a bike, learners instead ride bikes and work as a team to take them apart and rebuild them. All along the way are just-in-time interventions and lessons that teach specific historical, mathematical, scientific, or design principles.

Problem-based learning may seem like a simple concept that makes great common sense, but it is rarely deployed in K–12 and higher education. Although some K–12 schools have picked up on problem-based learning more quickly than institutions of higher education, across the gamut of educational experiences, this approach is more the exception than the rule.

Grand Challenges. One area that has been trying to reinvigorate problem-based learning is engineering education. In 2008, the National Academy of Engineering launched Grand Challenges for Engineering, a visionary model to prepare undergraduates to address "grand challenges" facing our society. The idea is that students don't just major in engineering but pick a global problem that moves them, such as making solar energy economical, providing access to clean water, securing cyberspace, restoring and improving urban infrastructure, developing carbon sequestration methods, engineering better medicines, or another one of 14 major problems. Each of these grand challenges naturally spans many disciplines, perspectives, and skills.

In the context of problem-based inquiry around how to prevent nuclear terror, for example, students learn the importance of different scientific and mathematical concepts while also developing their multidisciplinary, multicultural, and social consciousness competencies as well as entrepreneurship and business skills. In 2010, grand challenges became a major crux of President Barack Obama's "Strategy for American Innovation," and the National Academy's model was featured as an exemplar by the Office of Science and Technology Policy.[14]

Rather than front-loading the major with notoriously difficult classes, such as calculus, chemistry, and physics—also known as weed-out courses—the grand challenges model flips the experience so that learners spend more time transferring and applying that new knowledge through hands-on experimentation. "Students need to build," explains Jason Hyon, Chief Technologist of the Earth Science and Technology Directorate at NASA-Jet Propulsion Laboratory. "It's a training ground; 90 percent of problems come when you're building—failure in implementation, the wrong form factor. Everything works perfectly in theory and on paper. When you have to deliver a product, that's when you learn."[15]

Purpose Learning. Although the grand challenges model was designed for future engineers of the world, the framework is one that can apply just as easily to the humanities and other disciplines. Stanford d.school Executive Director Sarah Stein Greenberg has another name for it—*purpose learning*: "What if students declared missions not majors? Or even better, what if they applied to the School of Hunger or the School of Renewable Energy? These are real problems that society doesn't have answers to yet. Wouldn't that fuel their studies with some degree of urgency and meaning and real purpose that they don't yet have today?"[16] The d.school dreamed up a concept for the future of education in which students "declare a mission, not a major." Seven new labs (like the seven original Olympic Games) would bring together students from around the world to perform in-context research and application methods for moonshot goals, such as making clean water accessible to all citizens in water-scarce countries. There would be one lab working on hunger and another engaged in the hunt for alternative energy sources. And in the context of solving a larger, real-world problem, the boundaries between a math, anthropology, history, or social science department would ultimately make little sense and fade away.

Although these novel approaches make excellent common sense, many of them tend to favor younger learners immersed in learning full-time. In order to cultivate the best problem solvers in the world, purpose- or problem-based learning would start as early as elementary school and continue throughout our work lives. With stronger inquiry-based learning models available for people at more phases of their longer work lives, more working learners would be able to stay ahead of the curve and build new and emerging skills that translate into intellectual agility and workplace dexterity.

The Role of Virtual and Augmented Reality

More problem-based learning pathways are needed for millions more Americans. Over the course of a longer work life, learners will seek out educational modules that allow them to quickly acquire and demonstrate the skills employers want. In certain cases, learners will need to broaden their human skills; at other times, they'll need to acquire some vertical or technical expertise—or "plus" skills. But what exactly will those educational experiences look like for the new consumers of education?

This is where advancements in augmented reality (AR), virtual reality (VR), and simulations show great promise. Companies are starting to turn to AR and VR to train people in digital skills more rapidly and in real time. Digital skills, in particular, are a pain point for companies because tens of millions of Americans have limited to no such skills.[17] And that low level of digital literacy does not correspond to age. Both younger and older workers show limited ease with very basic digital tasks. The same is true for those with more advanced levels of education. For all of these reasons, companies like UPS, ExxonMobil, KFC, and BP are diving into VR and AR.

But even more interesting to examine is how some companies are leveraging immersive learning technologies for human skills development. Mursion is a learning solution that allows for scenario-based, deep learning. It is a leading provider of VR simulations focused on "soft" skills and leadership development. The company works with 100 major companies and educational institutions like Amazon, McKinsey, Education Testing Services, and Laureate Education.

Mursion, a riff on the word "immersion," delivers a platform that anyone can access on a computer. The platform combines live actors and AI to create immersive learning environments. The simulations replicate challenges that most workers confront on a daily basis, such as managing conflict, negotiating, and delivering feedback, and are designed so that learners can rehearse, practice, and improve their skills in a low-stakes environment.

In one simulation, you as the participant are dropped into a classroom and face five students. You're told that your job is to teach these children about the three branches of government. You immediately notice each of the kids shifting around, doing different things with their hands and eyes.

The platform relies on what Mursion has patented as its semiautomated digital puppetry control as well as a culturally adaptive avatar simulator. This enables a single human puppeteer to be all five of those children at once and come across differently and believably as a different child with different needs. The graphics are just good enough to let you read their body language. Each person has a different-sounding voice and a different way of holding themselves, moving, and reacting.

You can hear and sense their mood changes. You're given sufficient information—both verbal and nonverbal—so that you can react, adapt, and change your behavior.

Your performance is recorded, and after you interact with the avatars, you review it with a simulation specialist and receive feedback. The playback displays your video with ratings on speaking and listening, vocal fluency, engagement, and impact on avatars. Your coach shows you what you did well and what you could have done better.

Instead of withholding executive coaching for more seasoned professionals only, this human skills development empowers low-wage workers and everyone in between. Scenario-based training works especially well for leadership development, teaching, sales, and customer experience as well as training to overcome implicit bias. These sorts of simulations develop fluency in human skills by allowing working learners to practice the transfer of knowledge in virtual settings.

On-Ramps to Opportunity

On-ramps are another option for learners seeking just-in-time, human+ skills education. On-ramps are designed specifically to uplift adult learners and prepare them for jobs in demand in local labor markets. Built with employer needs in mind, they offer access to the right tools and training to develop digital fluency and transferable human skills as well as the relevant work experience that will lead to good jobs.

Through close partnerships with employers, on-ramps ensure that learners have the specific technical skills required for jobs in growing areas, such as health care, business and financial services, advanced manufacturing, and information technology. Program graduates are ready not only for the first job after their on-ramp but for the many other transitions they will face as their careers evolve.

The term "on-ramp" is simply a designation that Strada Institute for the Future of Work and Entangled Solutions use to categorize organizations with similar core features. Most of the groups gathered under this umbrella might not ever call themselves an on-ramp, but we use the term to group together a set of innovative organizations that are thinking critically about the pain points that have dogged underserved learners in the past. They include nonprofit organizations, for-profit providers, and workforce boards (regionally based entities charged with directing federal, state, and local funding to workforce development programs).[18]

Contextualized Learning. These tailor-made learning experiences prepare learners for specific work as well as the workplace that they will enter. Jewish Vocational Service (JVS) San Francisco, as an example, partners with University of California–San Francisco (UCSF), designing curricula and educational experiences to prepare program graduates for roles at the university. JVS incorporates employer-specific topics into the training, such as familiarity with UCSF's medical assistant software as well as on-site training. One JVS program, Excellence through Community Engagement & Learning, includes both classroom and paid on-the-job learning through an internship with UCSF.

Instruction in applied settings can be more conducive to retaining knowledge and skills than classroom-based instruction alone. Work-based learning eases the transition into a new role while confirming compatibility and boosting worker confidence before the official start date. As one learner explained, "It would be hard for somebody like UCSF to look at me and say, 'Oh, you have the necessary skills to work in a hospital setting.' The on-the-job training cycle has been very beneficial for me because I can maneuver to see what area I fit the best." Employees are then ready to contribute on day 1.

Experiential Learning. The on-ramp i.c.stars utilizes simulations to create problem-solving technologists of the future. Its rigorous four-month leadership and technology training program gives low-income learners close to 1,000 hours of training in preparation for work at leading technology service providers and then supports them for 20 months afterward as they transition to high-paying, full-time employment. More than 400 students age 18 to 27 who hold high school diplomas or GEDs and have six months of work experience vie for 20 spots each cycle.

A combination of an apprenticeship model with project-based learning, i.c.stars divides its cohorts into four teams that solve a real business challenge proposed by a partner company. Challenges range from building software to creating a mobile app prototype. Students learn general information technology skills, programming languages, and cybersecurity concepts on their way to becoming industry-certified professionals and gaining employment as entry-level programmers, business analysts, and quality assurance experts.

Sandee Kastrul, cofounder and CEO, explains how experiential learning is embedded throughout the entire four-month on-ramp:

> [E]very cohort of 20 is divided up into four teams. They form their own consulting companies and then they're competing with each other for the RFP to solve a solid business problem ... . Every cohort has a different Fortune 500 company that is their client. So today, we're building mobile apps; it was once websites and data projects, so it changes with the market and what the hot jobs are.
>
> And then we also have a mentor sponsor, which is a software development company that works with them through agile developments and is mentoring them one-to-one around software development. And I think the beauty in that design is that they're accountable to their clients, not their teacher. And so, we're shifting from school to work.

How it looks is you'd go to a client meeting, and you're presenting something, and lo and behold, something comes up. The client changes something. It's ugly. You have no idea what they're talking about. But you go and learn everything you can in order to meet those requirements. And so, we script all of these leadership objectives into the simulation, but the software that they develop is real.

And we don't want to put somebody in a track before they've had the opportunity to experience it. So, every one of the four sprints that they work on with their client, they're playing different roles. You might be a BA [business analyst] in the first sprint; you might be a developer in the second; you might be the scrum master in the third. And so, you're getting a taste of everything. And then during their last month, they're figuring out what made the most sense. What did I enjoy the most? What gave me the most fulfillment? And what am I really good at?[19]

Kastrul captures how an on-ramp like i.c.stars is able to teach leadership and technology at once. She views her learners as natural leaders in many cases because of the skills they have acquired in the face of adversity:

[W]e're going to need people who can walk between worlds, who can understand how to quickly adapt in a different given situation. And who better to walk between worlds and know how to adapt than residents in our inner cities, right? The world of school is different than home, different than work. We are constantly code switching, figuring out what unwritten rules are in any given situation. We have to be able to comprehend very quickly what's happening. And this is not just kind of like a deluxe thing; it is literally a matter of survival—that no matter what, these kids have overcome terrific adversity, and as a result of that, have developed all this resiliency.

Kastrul's thesis is that if she can teach programmers to lead, she can use their talent development as "a blueprint for solving the problems and building the solutions that are happening in our communities every day."

Tech-Enabled Skills Acquisition. On-ramps clearly do not focus only on technical skills. Colaberry founder Ram Katamaraja is quick to point out that in his data science on-ramp, human skills are just as critical. Colaberry is a data consulting firm that also operates a school of data science and analytics.

This on-ramp started with the idea of retraining military veterans and enabling their transition into data jobs in the civilian workforce. The initiative quickly evolved into trying to, as Katamaraja puts it, "figure out how to pass on the American dream to 100,000 people."[20] Through a unique AI-enabled platform, Refactored.ai, people can gain in-demand skills through a self-paced, interactive, learn-by-doing data science platform. They learn skills in structured query language, data analysis, data cleansing, data visualization, and applying algorithms. At the same time, participants regularly practice interview and presentation skills.

Colaberry won a 2018 MIT SOLVE "Most Promising Work of the Future" Solution award and has touched 5,000 learners from 45 different countries; 45 percent are women, and 70 percent are minorities.[21] Although the company does have learners with PhDs seeking to transition into new roles, for the most part, its learners hover around the poverty line. The company also partners with Year Up to work with young adults moving from data analyst internships to full-time employees in Silicon Valley companies. Out of all the learners who access Colaberry for an end-to-end program, 97 percent transition into full-time careers in the data industry.

Hybrid Learning Experiences. CEO Rebecca Taber explains that her organization, Merit America, is "taking folks from the working poor to middle-class careers."[22] Merit America learners have no more than a high school degree and are working full-time without benefits, trying to support families and kids on an average yearly salary of $27,000; 59 percent started college or community college but never finished, meaning that they also have some debt.

Taber asserts that it is "unrealistic for them to go back to college because they already tried that, and it didn't work for them. And just working their way up in the jobs they're in is also unrealistic because we have a really bifurcated economy right now, where there are a lot of jobs—where there is nowhere to go up." MeritAmerica therefore builds participants' skills so they can compete for jobs in IT, advanced manufacturing, and health care with $40,000 to $70,000 starting salaries and benefits.

To accomplish this, MeritAmerica provides hybrid learning experiences with lots of flexibility and plenty of intrusive in-person support. Intrusive advising is a positive form of support—intentional, high-touch contact to drive persistence and student success. Taber explains that the organization is "using technology and online learning for everything it does well, but complementing it with in-person support where we know online learning alone falls short."

The programs entail over 20 hours per week of technical skills building online. Learners complete that work asynchronously, without having to stick to a set class schedule—fitting the learning in whenever they can around their work schedules. Synchronous learning is saved for in-person squad meetings with five to ten peers and a Merit America coach.

In addition, every other week, participants meet one on one in person with a coach for a total of three hours. Each participant can pick a time from a range of options. The time together enables learners to discuss challenges they've faced with the technical lessons and also practice key professional skills, such as communication, conflict resolution, interviewing, and resume and cover letter writing. The programs range in duration from three to five months long. Early pilots have seen 80 percent completion rates, with 80 percent of graduates attaining new jobs within six months of finishing the program, and wage gains averaging $17,500.[23]

Wait ... Are These Bootcamps? Some of these programs initially sound like bootcamps. In 2014, we really started to hear about bootcamps, a vibrant new learning pathway for coding and software development skills. General Assembly, Flatiron School, and Hackbright Academy—to name a few—provided intense, experiential learning environments and were creating clear pathways to jobs, if not outright job placement. Learners paid anywhere from $10,000 to $25,000 to learn Ruby on Rails, HTML 5 and CSS, JavaScript, Agile Development, and other languages in intense eight- or 12-week periods. Afterward, they were ready to apply for developer positions at major technology companies.

In 2014, approximately 6,000 students graduated from a bootcamp.[24] By 2019, there were about 23,000 graduates in a market generating $309 million in gross revenue, according to Course Report, a site that tracks trends in coding education.[25] Major companies such as Facebook, Adobe, Etsy, Google, Goldman Sachs, and the New York Times have been recruiting proficient web developers from these brief, targeted programs.

Despite the hefty up-front, out-of-pocket costs for learners, thousands have flocked to coding bootcamps because of their strong outcomes. These programs boast job attainment rates that average around 82 percent, with notably high starting salaries that average $67,000. Some learners have even been able to attain six-figure salaries upon program completion.

Bootcamps have been proliferating and diversifying over time with new versions emerging in sales, data science, and even oil and gas. Author-investor Ryan Craig has dubbed these "last-mile" training providers exemplars of faster and cheaper alternatives to college.[26] Last-mile training providers are short-term, very targeted training programs that address skills bottlenecks in fast-growing technical fields.

In many ways, on-ramps leverage techniques similar to those of last-mile providers. Both kinds of programs address—head on—education and hiring frictions, but each addresses very different markets of learners and the employers that hire them. Bootcamps typically have not been designed to serve working-class adults. They have been neither priced nor structured to serve a population without an already high level of skills and education. Although some of these providers have experimented with serving adults without credentials, the 41 million working-class Americans do not comprise their primary market.

This is why on-ramps are such fascinating human+ skills-building models to keep an eye on. They are asking the right questions and providing sorely needed experimentation to determine what works in launching, reskilling, and upskilling our most vulnerable working learners.

Precision Education: Unlocking Modules of Learning

The decision to pursue a job transition is never easy and involves balancing competing priorities, interests, and risks. One-size-fits-all, cookie-cutter programs designed for 18- to 24-year-old students cannot and will not suffice for lifelong learners and prospective job seekers coming into their job search with different talents and specific upskilling needs. In order to help more adults successfully transition to their next job, career, and phase of life, it is critical that we build more modularized, targeted pathways.

A stunning 95 percent of workers report that they understand the value of lifelong learning, but that doesn't mean they'll want every element of a bundled, comprehensive degree program.[27] They'll need their education to be targeted, brief, and affordable—something they can complete in a short period to reduce time away from paid work and get them quickly into new, good jobs.

On-ramps are an amazing start, but in their early phases of development, they've not yet scaled widely enough. They only serve an estimated 100,000 learners per year out of a target population of 41 million working-age adults with less than a two-year degree; by comparison, community colleges serve approximately 1 million working-class adults annually.[28] We'll need more learning opportunities that meet learners where they are—more precise, short-burst opportunities that can fit into the mad, day-to-day hustle for survival.

Until now, employers have struggled to articulate and communicate the nature of the skills they value most, which heightens the challenge for educational institutions and training providers trying to keep pace with employer demand. States, regions, and organizations know precious little about the capabilities, aspirations, and potential of incumbent workers. Learners are unable to demonstrate to employers what they know and can do because they lack the right credentials or the signaling power of a degree.

At the same time, most employers and economic or workforce developers and policymakers haven't had actionable data to drive the creation of precision education and to allocate workforce dollars differently or more effectively. Although most intuitively understand that labor markets are hyperlocal, they don't know how this might alter their approach to talent and regional development and recruitment.

Today's technologies, however, offer a better view into the kinds of pathways that will enable workers to acquire the skills they need in order to advance in their work lives. With a finer-grained view of labor demand, as well as a better understanding of the career trajectories of millions of people in the labor market, we can begin to develop more targeted pathways to better opportunities.

Skill Shapes

A new vocabulary is emerging to fill the gaps between stakeholders in an increasingly complex labor market. Real-time labor market information, such as job postings and professional profiles, is being combined with cutting-edge analytical methods to provide a unique lens, which Strada Institute for the Future of Work and Emsi call *skill shapes*.[29]

The premise of a skill shape is simple: For example, most companies don't go looking for a computer programmer. They look for a software engineer and seek specific skills, such as structured query language, C#, or Javascript. And the shape of that role, or the different emphases on specific skills, varies based on whether an employer is seeking to fill that role in Wichita, Seattle, or St. Louis. At the same time, every single one of us has a unique skill shape; yours looks different from mine based on the knowledge, capabilities, and experiences we bring to the table.

A skill shape goes a step beyond traditional labor market data from government surveys to understand regional workforce needs. With federal taxonomies of industries and occupations updated only once or twice per decade, skills gaps often are identified at a broad occupation or industry level, such as a manufacturing shortage. Today, however, sources of "big," unstructured data—such as job postings and online professional profiles—can be updated as frequently as every few weeks to isolate actionable, real-time data. Although these data are not a silver bullet, they help us look underneath occupation and industry codes to gauge how employers are looking for specific skills, such as Six Sigma, machining, or Good Manufacturing Practices, for example, and how they compare to the supply of skills in a region.

Labor Markets Are Hyperlocal. Every skill shape is defined by its regional context. Some of the variation in skill demands can be attributed to differences in the kind of job openings offered by the unique set of employers in the region as well as by migration patterns, supply chains, and the regional supply of talent. Take a cybersecurity specialist as an example. (See Figure 7.1.)

In Washington, DC, knowledge of federal information security systems and protocols is the dominant skill, including a combination of fraud identification, hacking, and digital forensics, which commonly involves analyzing digital network vulnerabilities related to counterintelligence activities or law enforcement. In St. Louis, cybersecurity looks like a subset of data science, with advanced statistics, data modeling, and data visualization as more prominent skills. In Columbus, cybersecurity skills have a different emphasis.

When we layer on the skill shapes of the supply of talent in the region, we can easily detect where the skill gaps and surpluses are. (See Figure 7.2.) Let's look specifically at Columbus.

Columbus is becoming a hub for financial tech, particularly cybersecurity. Many of the skills associated with these roles are hybrid, requiring knowledge in both financial services and machine learning. But talent in the area is not keeping up with the demand for ethical hacking, intrusion detection and prevention, and network forensics. There is also a shortfall of talent in cloud computing, especially in Apache OpenOffice and Cassandra.

Skill shapes can expose skills gaps and surpluses for any region in any industry domain. Once policymakers, workforce and economic developers, learning providers, and employers understand their regional skills gaps, it becomes more obvious how to close those gaps and grow their local economies through the design and development of well-calibrated and more precise learning pathways.

Figure 7.1 In St. Louis, cybersecurity skills are oriented toward data analytics, while Columbus and Washington, DC, involve field-specific technical skills, such as ethical hacking and digital forensics.

Source: From Weise, Michelle R., Hanson, Andrew R., and Saleh, Yustina. The New Geography of Skills: Regional Skill Shapes for the New Learning Ecosystem. Indianapolis, IN: Strada Institute for the Future of Work, 2019.

Figure 7.2 The unique cybersecurity skills gaps in Columbus.

Source: From Weise, Michelle R., Hanson, Andrew R., and Saleh, Yustina. The New Geography of Skills: Regional Skill Shapes for the New Learning Ecosystem. Indianapolis, IN: Strada Institute for the Future of Work, 2019.

Ultimately, skill shapes provide the key to fulfilling the promise of competency-based education. We now have data to create truly modular and targeted pathways that can upskill and reskill employees to meet the needs of the local labor market. Especially in times of great economic upheaval, every region has the opportunity to identify and design the most critical and flexible modules in order to redeploy talent as rapidly as possible.

Education Becomes More Doable with Skill Shapes. Let's return to Jaylen's predicament presented at the beginning of this chapter and consider whether he really needs to get a degree. Based on a deeper understanding of the rapidly evolving manufacturing roles in Wichita, we can pinpoint the skills he needs in order to advance.

The skill shape of Wichita includes a mix of traditional engineering and business skills, such as forging, Aerospace Basic Quality System standards, and some aerospace engineering skills. Knowledge of lean manufacturing practices is critical, followed closely by a range of process improvement skills, such as Six Sigma, quality management, compliance, and corrective and preventive action.

Although it is a daunting list, by breaking the requirements down into discrete skills, as opposed to a more monolithic and time-intensive four-year degree, Jaylen can begin to chart a path forward to acquire these skills. He can also ask his managers which skills are most important to them. Suddenly, taking the next step seems a whole lot more feasible.

8 Integrated Earning and Learning

A new learning ecosystem must be **integrated**: Working learners need the time, the funding, the confidence, and the resources to integrate education and training with their existing responsibilities. A new learning ecosystem will reduce education friction and make advancement achievable by offering better funding options, new opportunities to learn while earning, and, ideally, more portable benefits.

What We're Hearing

Without a doubt, finances are a critical barrier for adult learners. "It's money," explained one woman. "When you're poor, you're poor."[1] Another interviewee described how she had trouble thinking about anything other than money: "My mental capacity's already full with thinking about how I'm gonna pay the bills, and next, how am I gonna find my work? How am I gonna do this? I don't have any more mental capacity to even think about trying to work on my own business or work on getting on LinkedIn to try to go through jobs and try to see what's out there. And so that is an obstacle. . . . There's so many things to keep the people who don't have a lot of money not having more money."

Our interviewees talked frequently about the "hustle." For one man, that meant having to stitch together part-time jobs on top of his full-time work. "I had my son at that point in time. So, then I just kept working, kept grinding, picking up other jobs, working two to three jobs, plus my full-time job . . . just to stay afloat." Another father explained, "You know, it's really been tough. I got one daughter in college and one getting ready to go, so it's money situations, you know? My hands are full, and I'll get frustrated because I can't concentrate on what I need to do to get to where I want to be."

The hustle simply takes over. One interviewee said, "Unfortunately, I always get put back into this place of where I'm hustling to survive and not necessarily [doing] the things that I truly, in my heart, want to do. So, I think that requires a bit of help because simply, I just don't have the time. But I know that the passion and the will is there to really change my life."

Adult learners consistently pointed to something bigger that prohibited them from putting their mental energies toward anything other than survival. One person kept repeating the word "survival." "Somehow, you have to try to navigate on your own. And a lot of times . . . I just keep going back to the word 'survival,' you know? We end up going into that place where we're scrambling in order to save our livelihoods, to save our homes, our apartments, our cars." Every day feels like a scramble or a mad dash for survival because, as one interviewee put it plainly, "In life, of course, everybody always has something going on. You're either going through something, about to go through something, or just came out of something."

Not Just About the Money

For adult learners looking to retool themselves, the cost of pursuing education extends far beyond the high price tag of postsecondary education or training. Education has other more palpable costs in terms of forgone wages and the tug on their most precious resource of all: time.

It's hard for working learners to imagine layering learning on top of everything else going on because they lack what a few interviewees referred to as "mental space." As one person said, "We all have a mental capacity with stuff that we can fill our brains with, and once you get to that capacity, you won't have any space for anything else . . . just having the mental space, the mental capacity to deal with everything."

Even when learners were ready to seek out education amid the hustle to survive, without "enough hours in a day," they admitted to feeling torn, unable to focus on school. One woman described her pattern of starting and then inevitably failing to persist because "it was a struggle, just the hours of having to sit in the classroom, when I had little kids at home, I was still working full-time. So it was again, another struggle, and years later, it was the same. I kind of fell back again."[2] The same thing happened for another woman who said, "My personal life kept making me get unfocused to be able to study and to stay in school. So, after two semesters, I dropped out of college again." There was no way for these women to focus and take the time to advance.

Inevitably, the struggle to survive in the near term with low-wage work supersedes the longer-term desire to pursue more education. Work inevitably takes precedence in order to provide for families, pay the rent, or pay for heat and gas. One woman explained the conundrum: "Working full-time would give me more freedoms in the moment that I felt were the priority. And graduating from college for me at the moment felt so distant, especially at a community college."

The lure of full-time work and the immediate monetary relief it provides pulls learners away from the exact activity that could enable their long-term social mobility. As one learner put it, "So I really felt like I need to go ahead and just jump into the market and start to make my way" instead of pursuing and paying for education. Another interviewee described how she decided to forgo her degree program because after starting out as a cashier in a major retail chain in Houston, she moved up to managing an outlet.[3] That seemed like the better move at the time, and it was—for a while. Unfortunately, she capped out at $31,000 per year and had more or less hit the ceiling of what she could expect to earn in retail and customer service—stuck without a way to move forward.

The Predicament: The Precious Resources of Time and Money

As much as working learners understand they need to acquire new skills and capabilities, the challenges of surviving on low wages while supporting the needs of others work against their best intentions. How can they possibly fit in extra learning—even if it's free—with the day-to-day struggle to survive? More broadly, we will all need to seek out opportunities to retool ourselves throughout our work lives, but how will we fit it into our busy lives?

The way things stand now, employers dangle traditional tuition reimbursement (TR) dollars as a human resources benefit that pays anywhere up to $5,250 for courses and fees associated with an education program from a regionally accredited institution. These are tax-deductible dollars for a company and a potential source of revenue for the participating college or university. But employers inevitably place most of the burden on employees to spend what little time they have away from work to pursue educational opportunities—all on their own as self-guided learners. Not surprisingly, a lot of these TR benefits go unused by employees.

Rachel Carlson, cofounder and CEO of Guild Education, saw an opening for these funds to be used to define and design programs for frontline workers to get the degrees and credentials they need for better-paying jobs. Major Fortune 1000 companies, such as Lowe's,

Walmart, Taco Bell, Discover, Lyft, and Chipotle, are now partnering with Guild to revamp their approach to developing frontline workers.

Guild solicits proposals from as many as 100 education providers (nearly all of them online) and curates the programs it deems best suited for the company. It negotiates with the universities on tuition discounts and facilitates the financial transactions between the employers and the schools, so that learners do not have to wait months to get reimbursed.

Guild then guides employees on finding the right programs and helping them pay. Together, they set goals and figure out strategies to manage their time. Student success coaches and advisors work with learners throughout the program—no matter the institution they're attending—all the way through graduation. Guild doesn't get paid unless learners are successful.

For colleges and universities, the pipeline of learners comes as a welcome relief. Schools typically spend between $4,000 and $6,000 to recruit a bachelor's degree student and up to $14,000 for a master's degree student.[4] The cost of working with Guild is cheaper than paying for students through those traditional channels.

Employers, too, benefit from investing directly in their employees' upskilling. "It's not only the right thing to do, to take care of people, but it also makes good business sense," Carlson explains.[5] Chipotle, for example, has observed that employees who leverage the TR benefit have a 90 percent higher retention rate than those who do not. Greater retention leads to less churn and greater cost savings by not having to continually hire and refill openings.

As exciting as innovations like Guild are, the premise of TR-related innovations relies on employees engaging in educational pathways *on top of* everything else they have going on in their lives—and outside of or in addition to work. The education frictions are immense.

In the future, the onus will be on employers to do more than offer TR as a nice-to-do human resources benefit for their employees. To facilitate long-life learning, companies will have to tap into and reimagine on-the-job training and redesign work-based, skills-building initiatives that extend far beyond getting employees compliant in sensitivity, antiharassment, or workplace safety training.

Learners need more hands-on opportunities while they are working to acquire the right skills for new, emerging, and better jobs. And those upskilling pathways need to be experiential and embedded into the workday because too much of the burden today rests on workers to skill up on their own.

In an age of continuous returns to learning, it is not sustainable to force adult learners who are struggling to survive to navigate their human+ skills development alone—on top of everything else going on in their lives. Working learners need skills-building experiences to meet them where they are and show them the abundant possibilities ahead.

Buying, Not Building, Talent

Unfortunately, "companies don't yet perceive middle-skills workers as strategic assets," explains Harvard Business School professor Joseph Fuller.[6] Indeed, 44 percent of employers offer *zero* upskilling or reskilling opportunities.[7] Employers consistently underestimate the talent they can cultivate inside their own workforce—a critical source of talent they'll need in the future.

From his survey, Fuller shows how business leaders frequently cite workers' fear of change as the main reason why they believe workers are not prepared for the future. But the attitudes of employees couldn't be more divergent. Most workers (three out of four) perceived the need to prepare for the future of work, while two out of three expressed confidence in their ability to prepare for that change. "As a result," Fuller concludes, "[employers] are not capitalizing on the widespread, latent optimism among their workers," nor are they positioning themselves to help workers develop the emerging as well as more durable skills needed in the face of automation.

What if, instead of spending an estimated $200 billion annually on talent middlemen, companies turned their attention toward their incumbent workforce?[8] Rather than consistently "buying" talent from outside of the company, employers could begin the hard work of building up their existing (and willing) employee base to address new and emerging forms of work. Imagine the collective impact if employers were to invest a fraction of that $200 billion directly into their incumbent workforce.

In August 2019, the Business Roundtable, an association of CEOs of American companies, produced a surprising statement redefining the purpose of a corporation as benefiting all stakeholders, including customers, employees, suppliers, and communities—not just shareholders. One part reads: "Investing in our employees. This starts with compensating them fairly and providing important benefits. It also includes supporting them through training and education that help develop new skills for a rapidly changing world. We foster diversity and inclusion, dignity and respect."[9] This is a broad and somewhat bland statement at first blush, but the idea of upholding employees as equal in importance to shareholders is powerful if the signatories turn these words into meaningful action.

By investing in their people and preparing them for the work ahead with continuous learning pathways and reskilling and upskilling opportunities, companies will not only demonstrate goodwill, but they will also ultimately serve corporate self-interest and survival. The businesses that begin building talent—instead of always buying talent—will win the talent wars of the future and reap dividends on their intermediate- and long-term competitiveness.

Funding Long-Life Learning

At the same time, the question remains: How are we going to pay for lifetime education? As we consider new funding models for lifelong learning, it's not as if there is a dearth of funding. There are estimates that over $1 trillion is being spent on postsecondary education and training, with colleges and universities spending over $400 billion and employers spending over $600 billion in employer-provided formal and informal training.[10] Private capital, too, is engaged in the heavy lifting, with over $40 billion invested in the education technology market in the United States alone, which includes early childhood, K–12, higher education, and lifelong learning.[11] The global EdTech market is expected to be worth $130 billion by 2025.[12]

Clearly, the postsecondary education and workforce training systems are flush with money. One would assume that more Americans would be thriving in the labor market. But in order to skill up Americans for the future of work, that $655 billion pot must be reevaluated.

Resources and services were not designed with a returning adult learner in mind. These systems, loaded with funding and innovations, can feel rigged to the most vulnerable learners and workers trying to keep up with a rapidly evolving knowledge economy. The OECD ranks the United States second to last among 29 developed nations in investing in taxpayer-funded training.[13] Although the Workforce Innovation and Opportunity Act was designed to help millions of Americans access the education, training, and support services they need in order to succeed in today's labor market, the federal investment nets out to the equivalent of $574 for each American seeking services from their regional workforce boards.[14] At the same time, most of the $177 billion in formal employer-provided training spending (58 percent) goes to workers with college degrees. Only 17 percent goes to workers with a high school education or less.[15] The lion's share of the roughly $246 billion of federal student aid issued each year goes to undergraduates, designed for learners at the front end of their adult lives, not middle-age workers seeking short-burst programs to reskill, upskill, and stay ahead of the tech curve.[16]

Venture capital, too, disproportionately flows to solutions aimed at the well educated, not the most underserved.[17] Most venture capital funding (75 percent), for example, flows to three states: California, New York, and Massachusetts.[18] According to one analysis, "From 2010 to 2014, five metro areas were responsible for half of successful business startups, and 73 of 3,000 counties generated half the job growth. The rest of America, including much of the working class, languished in distressed communities, where employment, income and business growth lagged well behind national averages."[19] The detrimental effects of the changes to come will be felt even more profoundly by smaller and less-well-educated communities.

Philanthropy, unfortunately, is not picking up the slack. Most philanthropic organizations are duplicating the efforts of their investor peers by attempting to catalyze innovation without any sort of coordination. There is relatively little transparency around the investments made by foundations and philanthropists. Rarely does one organization have visibility into the investments and grants being made by its near peers. Or, if some philanthropic organizations do reveal information about their grant making, there is no common taxonomy or consistent language that foundations use to describe their giving and the impact of those investments.

In her research for Entangled Solutions, Terah Crewes and her team pulled the 990 forms for every foundation in the country that gave over $5 million per year to education over a three-year period. This 2019 project yielded over 150,000 reports, which they submitted to natural language processing to break down where and how people were giving. Terms like "program development" emerged as one of the largest themes in the data, but because there was no clear definition of program development, it meant a range of things.

"The biggest thing that popped up when we were making sense and parsing through this data," Crewes explained in an interview, is that "most foundations are giving to early-stage development . . . the early stuff that catches the most media attention"—something akin to a seed-stage or angel investment in venture capital.[20] Much less money is going into scaling solutions. There is an expectation that these early-stage programs will ultimately become sustainable, but Crewes continues, "[W]e don't invest to help that sustainability happen," which "creates this really bad incentive to be focusing on the new, rather than scaling what works."

Whether it's federal funding, private capital, or philanthropy, funding mechanisms are not set up for long-life learning and are overlooking a huge swath of the American population who need the most help launching into promising, well-paying jobs and careers.

Seeds of Innovation: Making Time for and Funding Long-Life Learning

Let's first address the issue of time. Thankfully, some forward-thinking companies are beginning to view talent development as a business imperative, recognizing that employees lack the precious resource of time to juggle education and training on top of their existing responsibilities.

The retail giant Walmart recognizes that its 1 million employees lead complex lives outside of work. For that reason, the company saw the need to make training bite size, relevant, and integrated into the workday. It couldn't be constructed as a daunting load of activities *on top of* their people's existing responsibilities. Instead, learning had to be hands-on and connected in an obvious way to their future success.

The retailer therefore launched Walmart Academies to train 6,000 to 8,000 associates per week, leveraging training programs that rely heavily on virtual reality.[21] At all 5,000 of its retail stores, Walmart has virtual reality headsets available for training. Workers engage in three- to five-minute modules on the headsets, modules that typically take the learning experience design teams two months to create and vet. The use of technology (including iPads and the web) is paired with in-person training at facilities called Academy stores. Each Academy store offers 3,000 square feet of classroom space attached to high-performing Supercenter stores and trains an average of 25 other stores. Seventy percent of the training time is spent on the sales floor with hands-on learning. The incredible outcome of this $2.7 billion investment in the development of associates has shortened, in dramatic fashion, the timelines for implementing changes across all 5,000 stores—from six months to one week.

Beyond just near-term digital skills, Walmart is thinking about how to build skills on multiple fronts—for leveling, reskilling, upskilling, and beyond—across all levels of the organization, including senior management. The company is trying to shift the conversation from "training" to the concept that learning is continuous—24/7—and that everyone must learn new things and develop the muscle, so to speak, of embracing an agile mindset. Julie Murphy, Executive Vice President of People at Walmart, explains, "We need people to be comfortable with change, to be comfortable being uncomfortable." In her words, this work is critical because "getting people to embrace the future is fundamentally hard on confidence."

Practicing Human Skills on the Job

In that same vein of developing an agile mindset, some employers are also starting to realize that human or behavioral skills matter more than ever in terms of productivity as well as broader business outcomes.

A few have begun partnering with start-ups like GLEAC (Growing Leaders Entrepreneurship Academy for Creatives), which is experimenting with learning experiences to strengthen and practice human skills on the job. Founder Sallyann Della Casa launched GLEAC as an AI-driven skills assessment and training tool that teaches over 200 behavioral elements, such as persuasiveness, thinking on your feet, and altruism, as well as ten core workforce skills, including creativity, collaboration, and decision making.

Each GLEAC learning journey is specific to the user and job role with a focus on practicing the skills to make them stick. For employers, Della Casa explains, the upside is clear: "The power of an employer being able to understand the hidden strengths and/or learning agility of each [member] of its workforce is priceless in making business strategy decisions in the unpredictable world of work today."[22]

The first step is a baseline, individualized behavioral benchmark that acts as a GPS starting point, giving learners insight into their personal strengths and providing personalized guidelines on what to develop. Next comes a personalized micro-learning curriculum, which is structured and delivered as a series of daily practices that increase in difficulty. The learning is supported by ongoing coaching and feedback from peers.

According to Della Casa, this is where most online learning falls short. Learners need feedback on how others are applying those same skills in the same job situations. They also retake the behavioral benchmark every few months to validate skills development. Over time, learners and employers can assess an individual's development, in addition to understanding how the acquisition of those skills directly impacts the larger organization.

Prada and Accenture are using GLEAC to provide targeted training in the areas most critical to their workforce and clients. Della Casa explained that at Prada, for example, GLEAC's micro-learning was tangibly tied to key performance indicators around sales increases. One sales associate named Monica wrote on GLEAC's platform, "Today I had a customer walk in not looking like she had money to shop, but I remembered the lesson to not judge." That same customer ended up spending almost $5,000, said Della Casa: "This is a tangible outcome, a home run."

More important, the experience was seamlessly integrated into Monica's day so that she could learn while earning. GLEAC exemplifies the open opportunity for companies to embed smaller microinterventions that can take place during the workday and ultimately reduce education friction for working learners.

Funding Long-Life Learning

Now let's talk about financing continuous returns to learning. Critical to the welfare of working adults will be more options in terms of funding mechanisms.

Income share agreements (ISAs) are an emerging tool in the market, whereby students pay nothing up front to access additional education and pay back that investment only after completing the program, when they're working and earning. Repayment is intended to be manageable, so that once people are able to afford regular payments, they pay a fixed percentage of their earnings for a set period of time and usually with a cap on the total amount to be repaid. Done right, an ISA opens up schooling to all, without the risk of unmanageable, long-term debt.

Unlocking Economic Mobility through ISAs. The idea is to bank on a learner's future success as collateral to pay for education and training. For low-income and first-generation students (including disproportionately high shares of students of color, working students, and students supporting their own families), an ISA is a formal version of what their more privileged peers have access to—families who invest in their future human capital, financing education costs up front, without the fear of long-term debt.

The idea is potentially liberating—access to education beyond high school suddenly becomes affordable to everyone. Rather than taking on the risk of crippling student debt—now estimated at $1.64 trillion—students know their payments will be based on a fixed percentage of earnings.[23]

Tonio Sorrento, CEO of ISA provider Vemo Education, clarifies: "It's an idea of partnership versus debt . . . partnerships between schools and students. What we have is a better, more fair, more transparent form of tuition. You pay for success on tuition. Success is defined by you, the student, or your career path to keep score with outcomes. And the student and the school are on the same footing. You both succeed or fail together."[24]

If colleges and universities fund their own ISAs or contract with an ISA provider, such as Vemo or Leif, they have a vested interest in the outcomes of their students. If graduates find jobs that pay well, repayment is guaranteed and even accelerated. When graduates do not find good jobs, repayment is at risk, resulting in the loss of capital. The risk is effectively shared with schools. Aanand Radia of University Ventures calls it "a student loan with an insurance wrapper."[25]

More Transparency.   Income share agreements signal outcomes to learners and families. In the best version of themselves, explain researchers Andrew Kelly and Kevin James, ISAs create a "performance floor that would kick the worst-performing institutions out of federal aid programs, and a risk-sharing policy that would give institutions skin in the game."[26] The authors write that more transparency would also lead to new forms of learning outside of accredited institutions, validated for delivering on real outcomes, such as "direct assessments of student learning, increases in earnings potential, passage rates on relevant certification or licensure exams, and student satisfaction rates."

Sorrento adds that transparency about outcomes enables schools to compete with subpar schools that may invest a whole lot more in search engine optimization (being one of the top results to pop up in a Google search) or television ads with a call center to boot, with front-line call staff texting and calling students at all hours.[27]

Too Good to Be True? The devil is in the details. The terms of each ISA are important—minimum earnings threshold, percentage of income paid, caps on repayment duration, total amount repaid, as well as additional terms, such as life events that would qualify for forestalling repayment. And if the formula is unbalanced or unclear to students, what emerges on the other side could be less a tool for liberation than a new form of shackling students to debt.

Currently, neither state nor federal regulations govern ISAs. This emerging market is more like the Wild West, and early ISA providers are worried about the lack of regulation and the potential for one bad actor to sway the future adoption and growth of this new product. Without strong consumer protections and regulation, ISAs run the risk of burdening people with yet another debt to be serviced on top of their federal student loans, parent PLUS loans (federal aid for parents of dependent undergraduate students), and private loans.

Meanwhile, entrants in this market see ISAs as a potential trillion-dollar market to rival student loans, including servicing and secondary markets for bundling and selling ISA debt. This secondary market could spawn the creation of opaque financial instruments similar to the mortgage securitization and derivatives that contributed to the 2008 recession. Without greater clarity and regulatory frameworks, it is easy to imagine the proliferation of student debt speculation and its detrimental impact on learners.

If done right, however, the potential upsides to ISAs are tremendous, particularly for those who lack access to the promise of education to unlock economic mobility. Widespread adoption of ISAs could lead to a new era of transparency around earnings outcomes for both alternative learning providers and traditional colleges and universities.

More Skin in the Game.   A recurring theme in innovations in funding long-life learning is the idea that learning providers must get more skin in the game. With ISAs in a bit of a gray area at the moment, other approaches connected to income-based repayment are emerging.

Climb Hire relies on a funding model in which learners do not pay on the front end. "It's free to them," explains Nitzan Pelman, "but if they get a job that pays 45K or more, then they start to pay it forward for the next student, and that is in the cost of $150 a month for four years. It's not quite an [income share agreement] because it's a flat fee, and it's capped at exactly the cost of the program. So, it's $7,200. We don't take a penny more even if they could pay for longer."[28] Additionally, in this co-op model, program graduates become lifetime members of the organization and give back financially while also serving as mentors for new cohorts—a win for all stakeholders.

At i.c.stars, learners are paid throughout the four-month bootcamp as if it were a paid apprenticeship. Sandee Kastrul explains the need to provide substantial support: "That's just enough for transportation and food and whatnot because it's 12 hours a day . . . there's no way that you could go without any money, without big savings. And the folks who have big savings would not necessarily be an i.c.stars-profile person. And then in the residency, the two-year program, they're getting paid market wages. Whether they're working in our social enterprise, in our staffing business, or they went right to the market as W2 employees, they're earning technology wages."[29]

We'll explore more of these apprenticeship models in Chapter 9, but it's worth noting the new models cropping up to relieve learners from unfairly bearing all of the risk in their pursuit of education. In these models, learning providers share risk to ensure that their incentives are aligned with student success.

Career Impact Bonds

Tracy Palandjian, cofounder and CEO of Social Finance, an impact investing nonprofit, and her team have developed the UP Fund for upskilling America through career impact bonds. With a laser focus on low-income populations often locked out of high-quality education and training programs, career impact bonds are centered on the student, with safeguards built in and transparency around income thresholds, income share, payment caps, and grace periods.

Career impact bonds also come with a Student Bill of Rights and financial advising to ensure that learners fully understand the terms of the agreement with clear payment tables. They also cover the crucial wraparound services that learners need in addition to skills training.

Palandjian explained the critical need to create mechanisms for reapportioning risk. "Right now, all the risk is on the individual. And especially for people who are already struggling, who can't navigate in this uncertain world, why should they bear all the risk?"[30] Agnostic to the type of learning provider, the UP Fund underwrites organizations committed to offering promising pathways to low-income individuals, whether they are community colleges, coding bootcamps, for-profits, public workforce programs, or career technical education programs.

Outskilling. In a fascinating twist to rethinking funding models, FutureFit (one of the AI-based "skills compass" models we learned about in Chapter 5) is trying to carve out a business model centered on reimagining the future of layoffs. Because most businesses have distinct budget lines set aside for layoffs, FutureFit is looking to help corporations "outskill" those soon-to-be-laid-off workers—long before those pink slips arrive.

Leveraging AI, the platform pulls together skills assessments, job matching, career pathway recommendations, and education provider recommendations tailored to workers who need to develop new skills in preparation for that upcoming layoff. FutureFit hopes to ease the transition and prepare people for new jobs or even for entirely different fields.

Some companies are asking FutureFit founder Hamoon Ekhtiari to prepare for these tech-driven layoffs years in advance because, as *Wall Street Journal* reporter Lauren Weber explains, "Layoffs are morale-killers and make employers look heartless; companies are loath to take on the reputation risk. Federal and state governments have an interest in minimizing claims for unemployment insurance, and want to avoid the domino effects of laid-off workers cutting their spending, losing their homes, moving away or worse."[31] With massive displacement from a global pandemic and increasing automation on the horizon, we can expect to see more developments in this space and a reimagination of these particular funds dedicated to layoffs.

Lifelong Learning Accounts.   In an effort to translate lifelong learning into action, policymakers have been exploring lifelong learning accounts. There is a history of robust bipartisan support for legislation in this area in prior Congresses; both sides of the aisle have proposed legislation to create tax-advantaged lifelong learning accounts.[32]

Singapore's SkillsFuture work has garnered a lot of attention. It offers individual lifelong, top-up learning accounts for Singaporeans to access skills-based training to keep up with technological advancements and increased competition for jobs. Anyone over the age of 25 can use these government-subsidized accounts to pay for programs from a list of 500 approved providers. The government contributes to each account—$500 for younger learners and more for midcareer professionals. Hundreds of thousands of Singaporeans have already leveraged the SkillsFuture Credit to skill up.

In a similar vein, the Council for Adult and Experiential Learning here in the United States has developed and piloted multiple demonstration sites for Lifelong Learning Accounts (LiLAs) in Chicago, San Francisco, and New York City as well as in the states of Indiana, Maine, and Washington.[33] LiLAs are portable funds that stay with individuals regardless of where they are employed or if they are employed. Individuals contribute to the fund, and employers often match those funds. Other third-party sources can also contribute, including foundation or public sector funding and federal or state tax credits.

In the case of these demonstration sites, individuals were able to meet with education and career advisors to make informed decisions about the training and educational options aligned with their career goals. With a plan in place, learners used LiLA funds on tuition and fees, supplies, materials, and books. The ultimate aim of all of these test sites was to show why LiLAs should become a standard feature of employee compensation packages, with both employees and employers receiving tax benefits for contributions to these accounts that would finance continuous education and training.

As exemplified by Maine as early as 2005, creating LiLAs does not entail breakthrough innovations but often just a transformation of existing resources. The LiLA demonstration project was developed in concert with the Department of Labor and Career Center staff and offices. Those offices engaged in outreach to employers and workers while relying on Maine Centers for Women, Work and Community for educational planning support services. The LiLA funds were created through the state's existing 529 college savings program and included matching contributions from the state for low- and middle-income workers.

The Aspen Institute's Future of Work Initiative has been avidly following developments in the space and sees lifelong learning opportunities as a matter of public policy priority. In a 2018 brief, the Aspen Institute makes the case for Lifelong Learning and Training Accounts that would be funded by workers, employers, and the government. Anyone over the age of 18 would be able to contribute tax-deferred dollars (up to $10,000) into an account that would be matched by the government—with higher contributions allowed for low-income workers and no matching contributions for high-income workers. The authors explain that "79 percent of the cost of the proposal would benefit individuals who make under $30,000. . . . Once the balance has been drawn down, workers could replenish the account up to the overall limit."[34] Estimated costs to the government would be $25 billion over a ten-year period.

Not all workers will be able to depend on employers to help them update their skills over the course of a lifetime. They will need new ways of accessing financial assistance to support continuous skills building for the work of the future. Policy proposals for lifelong learning accounts can incentivize business and government to co-invest in talent development across a longer work life.

9 Transparent and Fairer Hiring

A new learning ecosystem must be **transparent**: The hiring process must be transparent, open, and fair—enabling job seekers to prove their competence and skills. When skills become the primary currency of the job market, employers will be able to access a more diverse pool of qualified candidates who have proved they have what it takes for the work ahead.

What We're Hearing

There has to be a lane in the labor market where someone can show what they can do, that their efforts lead to progress.

—Byron Auguste[1]

From the perspective of job seekers, the hiring process can be as baffling as it is frustrating. Intent on finding work, they can instead find themselves lost in a new world of algorithms and applicant tracking systems that determines their fate. One interviewee recounted: "I have spent so much time on ZipRecruiter and Glassdoor and Indeed. . . . The last time I actually had to go looking for a job, we did things like talk to people face to face, and that's completely gone now. You just submit your resume and cover letter via a website, and you never talk to anyone. There's no personality; there's no personalization of it. And you just end up getting put into a slot. And as a result, they don't know who you are." Because job seekers rarely hear back, they feel as if they exist in a vacuum: "You're not hearing from anyone, so you're not getting any feedback . . . no feedback whatsoever." Another interviewee described the system as a "complete black hole."

Or, in some cases, the job requirements are simply too steep and unrealistic for even entry-level roles. One young woman described the barriers she faced as she tried to become a psychiatric pharmaceutical sales rep. All of the jobs required at least "five years' experience, or you had to have an already existing network of physicians." Another shared that her search for entry-level roles consistently "required experience in related fields. I'm like, 'Well. I don't have any experience, you know?'"

In certain cases, job seekers struggle to be seen and get recognized by a hiring manager because they don't know how to market themselves or how to translate their skills into the language of the labor market. According to Ladders Inc., 71.6 percent of resumes miscommunicate skills acquired from previous work experience.[2]

One interviewee recounted that despite being valedictorian of his college class and a member of multiple honor societies, he couldn't get the role he wanted based on his education alone. "I probably applied for over 200 jobs in Silicon Valley, and I just couldn't get in. I was like, 'How do you get in?'"

The Predicament

Job seekers have very limited visibility into the practices of hiring managers. It's the employers who really have control of this part of the ecosystem. To illuminate the complexities of signal matching, or connecting the supply of talent to labor market demand, we'll shift our focus to employer perspectives and what we're hearing from them through various survey data.

Put simply, the matching process is not working. In 2019, seven out of ten employers reported that they were experiencing a talent shortage.[3] In a 2020 survey of 500 hiring managers conducted by the Chamber of Commerce Foundation, 59 percent of respondents stated that finding qualified candidates had become more difficult over the past three years.[4]

The disconnect between job seekers and jobs has a lot to do with the overreliance on formal credentials. The currency of today's labor market is, without a doubt, the credential. Degrees have become the coin of the realm. Employers are demanding more academic credentials for every kind of job. A phenomenon known as *upcredentialing*, or credential inflation, has seized the labor market. A college degree now serves as a proxy signal to communicate a job seeker's skill set and sometimes the de facto requisite for even low-level jobs.[5] According to one study, more than 6 million jobs now require a college credential that formerly did not require one.[6]

Moreover, when employers rely on a college degree as a primary signal, they often come up shorthanded, searching for something beyond the degree to signal a job seeker's true qualifications. Peter Cappelli of the Wharton School at the University of Pennsylvania points to job postings spinning out of control—packed with education and experience requirements that few applicants can meet.[7]

Bias, Bias Everywhere

These credential-based hiring practices filter out otherwise competent job candidates from the hiring process, creating barriers to entry for people with fewer economic and social advantages.[8] Prior to the pandemic, the organization Opportunity@Work had counted 71 million STARs, or low-wage workers "skilled through alternative routes" with the ability to perform higher-wage work, consistently being overlooked by employers because of this bias toward degrees.[9]

Unfortunately, solutions in artificial intelligence are not necessarily making hiring more transparent or fairer, as algorithm-based tools are vulnerable to gender and racial biases, which ultimately screen out potentially qualified job seekers and narrow opportunities to diversify the workplace. Moreover, innovations in workforce tech do not yet provide effective ways of extracting the necessary data in the screening process to see if someone is actually qualified for the work.

Adding humans to the equation doesn't necessarily improve the situation, since hiring tends to bring out some of our worst implicit and explicit biases. Research has revealed that we inadvertently disadvantage minorities and women without even realizing it. In fact, in scientific fields, both men and women view white male applicants as more competent and hirable than women.[10] All of these issues contribute to the inertia in diversifying lopsided or largely homogenous companies with dismally low numbers of women and minorities.

"I knew from personal experience," explained Vivek Ravisankar, CEO of HackerRank, a skills-based assessment platform, "that there are so many people out there who are more than qualified for a job but get overlooked because they didn't go to a top school, don't have a fancy degree or a high GPA or don't have the connections to get their foot in the door. It was clear to me that hiring is broken—the skills gap is really a pipeline problem. Hiring should be based on skill, not pedigree."[11]

Inching Toward Skills

A growing number of companies are beginning to rethink their hiring and recruiting practices—shifting their emphasis to skills. In the same Chamber of Commerce Foundation survey mentioned earlier, 78 percent of respondents reported that "they will need to reassess the way they hire in order to find suitable candidates," and 67 percent are looking to incorporate skills assessments into their interview process.[12] Another survey from LinkedIn finds that "69 percent of professionals think verified skills are more important than college education when job-seeking and 77 percent of hirers agree they are investing more towards hiring based on applicants' skills or competencies."[13]

It's important to note that these skills are not confined just to technical or "hard" skills; employers are increasingly sounding the call for human skills. Jamai Blivin, founder and CEO of Innovate+Educate, works with employers to implement competency-based hiring programs and explains, "We kept hearing from employers that 'soft skills' were the problem," including "critical thinking, communications, customer service, adaptability, and drive for results."[14]

Momentum appears to be building around skills-based hiring, but the practice is still uncommon enough to be newsworthy. In 2019, Ginni Rometty, executive chairman of IBM, told reporters at a Business Roundtable event that "skills matter as much as a degree." She continued, "The only way to a good-paying job cannot be a four-year degree."[15] IBM is one of a few major employers, including Google, Starbucks, Apple, and Hilton, that no longer require a degree for well-paying professions.[16]

New hiring approaches are just beginning to emerge, and it's difficult to discern how much is hype and how much is connected to real action. Although nine out of ten employers say they are open to hiring a candidate without a four-year degree, the data on hiring just doesn't back this up yet.[17] A 2018 report from Northeastern University's Center for the Future of Higher Education and Talent Strategy found that only 23 percent of respondents are moving toward skills-based hiring.[18]

This may have something to do with the historical absence of more precise ways of quickly cutting through the jungle of resumes, cover letters, and LinkedIn profiles that employers must traverse to assess the qualifications and attractiveness of prospective employees—not to mention the roughly 738,000 unique credentials that have flooded the education and labor markets.[19]

The Assessment Void

The efforts to move toward skills-based hiring have also been stymied by a lack of robust assessments in postsecondary education and workforce training. Most tests get at what mathematician and philosopher Alfred North Whitehead called "inert knowledge," the kind of knowledge and theory that disappears rapidly from our brains because it is not applied in real-world contexts.[20]

To illustrate the fleeting nature of inert knowledge, Lawrenceville Academy, a prestigious boarding school in New Jersey, performed an interesting test: Returning students from two different years of high school were asked to retake the same science final they had taken just three months earlier.[22] The average grade of B+ dropped to an F. Not a single student had retained any of the major concepts they had presumably mastered just a few months prior.

Sadly, the vast majority of our tests and certifications are centered on this kind of knowledge, which fails to stick. Take an exam like the SAT, which purportedly tests critical-thinking skills. "The way that you succeed in this test is knowing the ways in which they've standardized it," explains Michael Price, an SAT tutor featured in the 2015 documentary *Most Likely to Succeed*.[21] "They've made it predictable, and you have to then behave in a predictable manner."

Reliable assessments of learning or applied knowledge are hard to find. Researchers from Ithaka S+R, a higher education research and evaluation nonprofit, describe the talent marketplace as a virtual "Wild West of pre-hire assessment" flooded with screening technologies.[22] There is a kind of anarchic quality to the flurry of third-party providers touting "high predictive capabilities and verified job matching abilities" with little basic science research or critical peer review to verify these claims.

It is unclear whether these assessments are measuring what matters. Deep learning is slow learning. It also involves struggle, not ease of mastery, and that struggle doesn't show up well on tests. As author David Epstein explains, "The most effective learning looks inefficient; it looks like falling behind."[23] Epstein synthesizes a huge body of work by cognitive psychologists that demonstrates that lasting knowledge and better performance later in life comes with poor performance in the near term. Deep learning "is best done slowly."

Hiring managers, meanwhile, desperate for ways to filter and sort through candidates and fill openings as expediently as possible, are turning to these unproven assessment tech companies. In a 2017 survey of more than 800 human resources professionals, more than half were using assessments as part of the hiring process—most of them delivered online.[24]

Seeds of Innovation: Toward Skills-Based Hiring

When the TV show *The Voice* premiered in 2011, it distinguished itself from other televised singing contests by featuring a blind auditions phase. Contestants had 30 seconds to sing their hearts out while four rock star judges sat with their backs turned to them. During that short interlude, each person had the opportunity to lure one or more judges to turn their chairs around based on voice only. Nothing else mattered.

The concept of the blind audition really came to the fore in the 1970s when major orchestras started implementing them. In 1970, fewer than 5 percent of the players in the top five symphony orchestras were women.[25] Once orchestras began putting up a curtain between the player and the jury, the outcomes changed dramatically. To further reduce any potential bias, players had to take their shoes off, so that the sound of heels didn't predispose the judges. It worked. Researchers have concluded that implementing blind auditions in the first stage of the audition process increases the odds for women by 50 percent.

Innovators are now experimenting with how to bring more blind auditions to the labor market. New entrants are building assessments and platforms to position a wider range of people as promising contenders in the workforce. We'll begin by looking at some novel forms of testing and move to other forms of democratizing the hiring process.

Blind Auditions for the Workforce

"If you want to know what a person knows and can do," explains former Dean of Stanford University's Graduate School of Education, Richard Shavelson, "sample tasks from the domain in which that person is to act, observe her performance, and infer competence and learning."[26]

This is what psychometricians call the criterion-sampling approach. Shavelson was part of the Council for Aid to Education's efforts to create the Collegiate Learning Assessment (CLA), a test to measure human capabilities differently than the SAT or ACT. The intent of CLA was to measure broader competencies, such as critical thinking and problem solving, rather than the accumulation of mere content knowledge.

A core feature of the CLA is a 90-minute performance-based task with a prompt and an accompanying set of background documents. This portion of the exam is well known in academic circles because of something called the DynaTech performance task.[27]

The prompt goes something like this: You (test taker) are the assistant to the president of DynaTech, a company that makes aircraft instruments. The president was about to acquire a plane called the SwiftAir 235, so that she and other business development managers in the company could use the aircraft to visit clients. Just before the purchase, a SwiftAir 235 crashed. Your job is to sift through an assortment of documents, such as newspaper articles, data and charts, the federal accident report, emails, analyses, and photos—some of which are relevant and some of which may not be—to inform your president's decision-making process. The end result should be a prepared memo that "addresses several questions, including what data support or refute the claim that the type of wing on the SwiftAir 235 leads to more in-flight breakups, what other factors might have contributed to the accident and should be taken into account, and your overall recommendation about whether or not DynaTech should purchase the plane."

This exam was designed to be taken at the end of a college education, but its application extends far beyond that rite of passage. It's unfortunate that more employers don't know about this test, because a person who can think through a problem like this is likely someone with strong, real-world problem-solving chops. What employer wouldn't want an employee who can synthesize information, evaluate a situation, exercise judgment, and convey clearly what should be done? This task embodies the act of critical thinking in a highly ambiguous circumstance.

The Council for Aid to Education has since teamed up with another assessment company, called Authess, which also uses situational judgment exams, to create SkillMetric, an hour-long exam made up of two 30-minute tasks that identify workforce readiness and talent by measuring critical thinking skills. With SkillMetric, the CLA exam is condensed and combined with benchmarking tools from Authess. A test taker's answers are compared with responses from industry professionals who have also taken the same scenario-based assessment. SkillMetric users are then categorized in terms of levels of mastery: emerging, developing, proficient, accomplished, or advanced.

Measuring What Matters. A venture-backed assessment company called Imbellus is taking scenario-based assessments to another level in its aspiration to measure how people think and how to measure curiosity, problem solving, systems thinking, and risk taking—abilities and aptitudes that have been nearly impossible to capture through bubble tests but also the very ones that employers have signaled interest in.

Each test taker is transported into a virtual setting to solve a broad challenge. The assessment does not test the content knowledge that learners come in with. Learners need no background information in biology, for example. Imbellus CEO Rebecca Kantar explains, "We're not looking at, did you learn this thing from biology class? We're looking at, here's a bunch of information; here's a problem. How do you come in, digest that information, and come up with a solution? It's all about how you use what's self-contained in the assessment. It's a closed-loop ecosystem."[28]

Through simulations built within natural world settings, learners encounter a disease that is spreading. It's their job to figure out how it's spreading and who's going to be infected next. They have to figure out the rules governing the disease in order to develop a treatment plan to prevent it from spreading further and to treat those already infected. The back end of the technology measures every click, mouse movement, and time stamp in order to make inferences about participants' information-processing, decision-making, and problem-solving skills—how they make choices and how they think through problems.

The system constantly gives feedback in this more fluid and dynamic experience. Learners make a choice, and the system responds and gives more feedback. Learners toggle through different data and, again, the system responds from the choices selected. Kantar describes the process of analyzing each move as part of a larger assessment:

> We have to create the equivalent of those question-by-question items [in a traditional multiple-choice exam] by looking at this stream of data—what you collect, what you looked at, how long you clicked on it, the order of your events. Every mouse stroke,

every click, and movement for us is data that helps us get a front-row seat to really three aspects of your behaviors that we're interested in. The first is really around research. Do you take advantage of using the information that is provided to you? That's a kind of a bucket of scores that we try and derive from that data—how well were you taking advantage of the information? Another bucket is more around these process scores as we call them. How do you parse information? How do you come up with new ideas? How do you make a decision? Do we see evidence of you doing a risk-reward calculation? What do you leave behind that gives us a lens into how you were thinking about things? And then there's a final bucket, which is: What does your final set of solutions really look like, and how sound were those?

Imbellus is a game simulation that directly engages learners in problem-based learning and "what happens to humanity based on the choices [they] make."[29]

These seeds of innovation underscore the need to move beyond measures of inert knowledge, which is much easier to quantify but yields such meager returns. In a longer work life, we'll need more assessments of deep learning.

Better Matchmaking Tools. While we wait for more innovations in the assessment space, other innovators, such as the start-up Skillist, are working on a skills-based job application platform to match candidates without a four-year degree to open jobs. Skillist brings to the fore the key skills from a job posting and simultaneously asks thousands of job seekers to generate their own related, matching skills with real-life workplace examples.[30] Candidates prove they have the skills by illustrating the last time they demonstrated or performed x or y skill. The platform then marries the supply of new and diverse resumes to the employer seeking those precise skills.

Most important, to blind the initial screening process for hiring managers, the platform de-identifies and standardizes the resumes and shows only evidence-based examples of skills. Removing personal identifiers mitigates bias and enables hiring managers to evaluate candidates fairly on what they can *do* rather than on who they are or where they come from. Once a manager has reviewed the people on the identity-blind platform and chosen whom they want to contact, those candidates are moved seamlessly into the employer's existing applicant tracking system or recruiting workflow, where they can be scheduled for a phone screen or in-person interview.

With an applicant-to-offer rate four times higher than typical resume-based hiring, Skillist's tech platform was acquired by Opportunity@Work in 2020 to give millions more Americans, skilled through alternative routes, a fair shot in the job market.

Blinded, Performance-Based Internships. A company called Parker Dewey has created new talent pipelines for employers through a digital micro-internship platform. Deconstructing the idea of a summer-long, in-person internship, Parker Dewey helps companies turn tasks that generally require the skills of an intern (or a task that is *not* the best use of a leader's or team's time) into discrete, micro-internship projects priced anywhere from $200 to $600 per task.[31] These short-term tasks can be done remotely and might include finding 50 leads in a defined market, drafting blog posts and social media content, engaging in market research, or identifying key influencers or top candidates for open roles. Posting a task takes only a few minutes. Employers then pick their interns from profiles in the marketplace and "test drive" the learners' skills and fit through short-term assignments.

Most learners come from public and less selective institutions, and through the platform, they are able to gain real-world work experience to launch into careers after school more successfully. Businesses win, too, by hiring from a broader talent pool and realizing that they can access a much more diverse candidate base without an elite pedigree to solve their business needs.

Communicating What You Know: A Can-Do Hub

All of these innovations in workforce tech, from assessments to skills-based hiring platforms, show how people need better ways of not only developing an accurate picture of their strengths and skills but also sending clearer signals to managers and recruiters about all that they can do.

Employers, too, need simpler ways of teasing out insights about the skills of job candidates and all of the learning that occurs both within and beyond traditional institutions of higher education. They need crisper ways of visualizing workers' profiles in order to do a better job of matching people with jobs.

In today's economy, badges, microcredentials, and certificates have aimed to bridge the gap, but they leave a lot to be desired. While human resources departments are eager for better "people analytics," that concept is still fuzzy. Simply collecting data is not enough. To be used, data has to be presented usefully.

One potential analogical model is GitHub, a social networking site for web developers to collaborate on open source code management. It's a way for developers to display their revisions of public repositories of code. Anyone in tech will recognize the grid in Figure 9.1 as a GitHub user contribution graph. The darker the shading, the more a person has contributed to the platform.

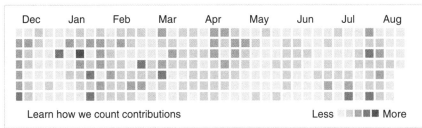

Figure 9.1 Anonymized user profile sourced from GitHub.

Source: From GitHub

I'm more interested in GitHub for how it visualizes skills than how it serves as a way of sharing public contributions. Imagine using a profile like Figure 9.1 to visualize competencies. An employer could immediately see the depth of a candidate's abilities in different areas—both her human skills as well as her other technical skill sets.

What if we could click on that darker-colored square in the grid and immediately view the artifacts from the candidate's past experiences that best illustrate that competency? Or, in other cases, we might see that a company or institution validated that particular competency. A profile of competencies with the visual impact of a GitHub graphic would immediately make clear to employers a candidate's capacity and potential. At the same time, each person would be able to identify the gaps in their skills.

Using a grid such as this, employers and managers could access a candidate's or employee's profile and get a more granular, complete view or could zero in on the skill sets and competencies that are most important to them. The grid could toggle accordingly to show the depth of the person's experience and growth over time. Employers would be able to scan quickly and see the strengthening and deepening of a person's abilities.

Ideally, this would also be a social network and e-portfolio, allowing an employer to see samples of work and to trust that the skills presented had been validated by others. (The social component of GitHub is important to underscore because other developers validate and consume one another's work. This contrasts starkly with the "skills"—if we can call them that—that users can tag so quickly on LinkedIn, such as "higher education" or even "ninja.")

A tool like this could have an impact far beyond hiring better candidates or getting a clearer picture of an employee's skills. It could even lay the groundwork for a marketplace that didn't have to depend so heavily on college degrees as proxies for talent. A can-do hub would reset the long-broken dialogue between industry and education and enable more direct connections between learners and the jobs they desire.

Getting Clear on Skills

Ultimately, when skills become the central focus, there can be greater clarity and efficiency in hiring. Job postings can be stripped of degree requirements. When employers give up the shorthand of a college degree, they have a new opportunity to get specific—and realistic—about what they most want in a hire.

Andy Seth, the CEO of Flow, a digital marketing agency, finds that a sharper focus on skills has made hiring easier and quicker. "Now my hiring is so much faster. Initially it took me time to figure out how to use skills-based practices and then translate each job description into that. But it served as a way to get clear so that my decision making and hiring became easy."[32]

In a skills-based world, resumes don't need names, addresses, years of experience, and other information that provides hints or adds bias to the screening process. Alternatively, hiring managers can limit the relevant years of desirable experience for the position—say, zero to one year for an entry-level position—or they can allow applicants to describe their relevant experience from the previous ten to 15 years for more senior-level roles to avoid age discrimination. They can also rely on structured interviews and phone screening protocols while leveraging "blinding" technologies to prevent phone screeners or interviewers from knowing the age, gender, race, or ethnicity of the applicant.

These sorts of blinding tools and technologies will not only save time and money during the recruitment process but can also improve the long-term return on investment of hiring decisions. One twist on skills-based hiring is something known as *open hiring*. Developed by

Greyston Bakery, it opens job opportunities to anyone who can meet a basic set of requirements.

As an example, job seekers looking for work at The Body Shop's warehouses simply have to meet the physical requirements of warehouse work (i.e., standing and lifting). After The Body Shop piloted the practice, monthly turnover in the distribution center dropped by 60 percent. Open hiring has been shown to reduce churn, ultimately saving employers time and money and freeing up more funds for training, benefits, and support for employee needs, such as transportation.[33]

"Try Before You Buy"

Hiring comes with risks: Recruitment and onboarding employees is expensive—approximately $4,000 per employee—and high churn rates can quickly escalate these costs.[34] Businesses are eager to reduce the cost of bad hires, which they understand in terms of added recruitment costs, productivity problems, and the potential costs and complexities of letting ineffective workers go. Because many employers may simply refrain from hiring when they can't easily identify talent, innovators are experimenting with new models to mitigate risk in the hiring process.

New "try before you buy" outsourced apprenticeship models make it easy for employers to test-drive applicants as they reach out to a more diverse talent pool. Once a candidate has proved him- or herself, the hiring process becomes more of a formality.

Apprenticeships are regarded as the gold standard of work-based learning. Highly effective modes of career preparation, apprenticeships include a mix of formal training and informal learning on the job, including a training wage. Although presidential administrations on both sides of the aisle have supported expanding and modernizing apprenticeships to serve high-growth industries and occupations, few models address areas beyond the traditional building and industrial trades. Techtonic is one of those few programs.

A software development company based in Denver, Techtonic also operates an IT apprenticeship program now certified by the Department of Labor. "We pay people on day 1," CEO Heather Terenzio explains.[35] "People walk in the door with no skills and they start getting paid to learn how to be software developers." Screened candidates complete 12 weeks of training, akin to a coding bootcamp. Techtonic's learners are predominantly women, minorities, and veterans—everyone "from GED students to baristas to Uber drivers to 'I was an Ancient Greek history major and I want a career in software development,'" Terenzio says.

After learners finish their training, Techtonic hires them, pays them entry-level wages, and pairs them with senior developers. During this period, trainees work on projects for firms at which they eventually hope to find full-time employment. While apprentices are being paid for their work, they simultaneously develop and hone skills they will need for long-term career success. At the same time, Techtonic's client firms have a seamless, low-stakes way of evaluating a candidate's work before committing to full-time employment.

Unlike a traditional apprenticeship in which the trainee is hired directly by a firm, this outsourced apprenticeship makes the on-ramp (Techtonic) the employer of record, and the firm a client of the on-ramp. Apprentices work for the firm that will eventually hire them, but they do so off-site while being managed by Techtonic. "In these models, apprentices sit at the service provider doing client work, proving their ability to do the job, reducing hiring friction with every passing day until they're hired by clients," says Ryan Craig, author of *A New U*.[36]

Through this model, employers can widen the playing field to include people without college degrees. Terenzio has always questioned the bias toward degrees: "I always have in the back of my mind that you could learn software development without having a college degree . . . some of the best software developers I had ever known over the course of my career were English majors and taught themselves how to code or didn't even go to college or didn't finish college."[37] Employer partners, too, are now recognizing that through these partnerships, they can begin to rethink their preference for degrees and build more diverse talent pipelines.

Test-Driving Talent. LaunchCode operates a similar try-before-you-buy model for people who are underrepresented in the technology industry.[38] Learners engage in an introductory 20- to 30-hour online curriculum, delivered in tandem with community partners, such as public libraries. They then enter the core program, which blends online and face-to-face learning over a 14- to 24-week period.

LaunchCode ultimately hires and manages their graduating participants as apprentices and sells their services to other businesses for $35 per hour. After a 90-day paid apprenticeship, the employer for whom the trainee was working determines whether they will hire the apprentice as a full-time employee. LaunchCode graduates receive an average salary increase of 200 percent.

Kenzie Academy, based in Indianapolis, offers a similarly fascinating two-year program melding a coding bootcamp with an apprenticeship model.[39] Learners range in age from 19 to 52, and 50 percent of them do not have a college degree. Many are veterans, stay-at-home mothers, or recently laid-off workers looking to reenter the workforce.

During their first year, learners are immersed in software development full-time. They pay $24,000, often using an income share agreement. During the second year, however, the $24,000 cost of the program is covered by the learner working for Kenzie Studios as an apprentice. Apprentices are paid $20 per hour to take on projects for different employers. Kenzie also offers shorter-term bootcamps in user experience, DevOps (software development + information technology operations), and digital marketing.

Participants in these various outsourced apprenticeship models learn skills in context and get to know an employer's culture while they are earning money. This approach not only smoothes hiring frictions by reducing risk for employers engaging with less conventional talent pools, but it also allows apprentices to test out the culture of a potential future employer. The learning providers also win by developing a more consistent revenue model, not wholly dependent on funders or philanthropists.

Although these are fascinating developments, these try-before-you-buy models are still very much seeds of innovation. Outsourced apprenticeships are anomalies in an already small pathway of apprenticeship opportunities in the United States. Only 585,000 Americans enroll in 23,000 registered apprenticeships each year, compared to the 26 million students enrolled in two- and four-year colleges.[40]

Widening the Talent Funnel

All of these blinded, skills-based hiring practices empower employers with new strategies not only to assess and validate the competencies that job seekers offer but also to translate buzzwords like "diversity," "equity," and "inclusion" into action. Increasing the diversity of the workforce has been shown to promote innovation and improve performance. Workers with varied perspectives can strengthen the workplaces of the future.

Economists Raj Chetty and Alex Bell have made this clear through their research on "lost Einsteins," in which they assert that "if women, minorities, and children from low-income families invent at the same rate as high-income white men, the innovation rate would quadruple."[41] A 2012 National Center for Women & Information Technology study on women's participation in information technology patents found that patents with mixed-gender teams were cited 30 to 40 percent more than similar patents with all-male teams.[42]

At Barclay's, Director of Cybersecurity Wayne Kunow explains that hiring diverse talent "means reflecting the customer base, which equals better customer experience." He characterizes the widening of talent pipelines as priceless, based on his work with Per Scholas, a free information technology training on-ramp for underserved Americans:

> Most firms are looking for experienced people almost all the time, and they want a certain recognition. They want a certain skill set, and they don't want to settle for anything less than that. And do you know what the reality is? There are some jobs where that is correct; however, I would propose to you that you could hire somebody that has the basic skill set, the will, and the desire to learn, and really wants to make an impact. You can hire someone who does not have all of that experience, and you'll get the results that you're looking for within a relatively short period of time. And while they're getting up to speed, they're still going to be productive and providing valuable services to Barclay's. That to me is factual because I've done it time and again. I've hired people from Per Scholas.
>
> I'm thinking of Tanzee [an on-ramp participant]. . . . The people that hired him, or some of them anyway, said, "Oh, this is not going to work because we can't hire a storage person because it's an experience skill set, and he didn't have the skill set. He's only got a basic skill set." Well, fast forward to two years into it, he's had multiple certifications on the infrastructure that he worked on because he wanted to learn, and he has more certifications than probably the people who were saying that he wasn't going to be able to do it. . . .
>
> I can use another example, which is Ivan, one of my favorites. Ivan was working so hard and just kept soaking it up—was doing stuff of an experienced engineer that's probably had seven or so years' experience. He was doing that in about six months into his tenure at Barclays. When you think about things like that, can I put numbers and dollars and cents to that?[43]

The return on investment is clear to the employers engaged in a deliberate diversification of talent pipelines. They can connect to the invisible talent pool in their midst and effectively win by building a more inclusive workforce.

Each of these seeds of innovation shows us that making the hiring process fairer can empower all learners, regardless of their starting point—race, zip code, or family income—to compete for promising opportunities.

10 Getting Started: Taking Root

A new learning ecosystem must connect all five of the guiding principles to serve working learners better. Long-life learning depends on stakeholders, resources, solutions, and services all coming together in a way that is at once navigable, supportive, targeted, seamless, and transparent.

In Richfield, Utah, in Fishlake National Forest, there is a 13-million-pound giant called Pando, which means "I spread" in Latin. Pando is a mass of 47,000 identical aspen trees with a singular root system stretching over 106 acres.[1] It is purportedly the largest living organism on earth.[2] That single root system is a complex set of highways that links every tree together.

Suzanne Simard is a forest researcher who has written about these dense networks belowground. In a popular TED talk on the secret communication of trees, she sheds light on this whole "other world," as she describes it, the "massive belowground communications network" of fungal highways that connect trees to one another.[3]

Trees that might appear to be competing for resources are actually secretly coordinating in sophisticated ways invisible to us. Humans can spot mushrooms above the earth, but those "are just the tip of the iceberg," explains Simard. What we can't see are the thousands of strands of fungal threads (mycelium) taking over the roots of trees and plants. "The web is so dense," she explains, "that there can be hundreds of kilometers of mycelium under a single footstep. And not only that, that mycelium connects different individuals in the forest . . . and it works kind of like the Internet." Through mycorrhizal networks, Simard has been able to show how a paper birch can converse with a Douglas fir through their back-and-forth transfer of carbon, nitrogen, phosphorus, water, and even defense signals. Nutrients are traded in "a lively two-way conversation."

The dense network of communication is deeply strategic. If a seedling is more shaded, more nutrients will be transferred to it to counteract barriers to growth. Trees even recognize their own kin—mother trees will send more nutrients to their seedlings and can increase seedling survival by up to four times. Simard summarizes: "Underground there is this other world, a world of infinite biological pathways that connect trees and allow them to communicate and allow the forest to behave as though it's a single organism. It might remind you of a sort of intelligence."

The Data to Knit It All Together

This incredible root structure makes obvious the work ahead in creating a better-functioning learning ecosystem. The systems of learning and work exhibit nothing close to the connectedness of a natural ecosystem, for we lack the fundamental elements of a strong data infrastructure.

Amazon, Google, Tencent, and Netflix, in contrast, use impressive closed loops of data, a continuous learning model. Every single click, page view, choice, purchase, and review is housed in the same system. These companies stand out because of the breadth, depth, and connectedness of their data. The amount and types of data that can be ingested, analyzed, and utilized is massive.[4] The companies know exactly who their customers are; where they went before, after, and during their visit; and everything they saw along the way. Every time we ignore, choose, or dismiss a suggestion, the selection is registered as more data. A closed loop of data leads to the creation of a flywheel or virtuous cycle of continuous improvement.

When we transfer this closed-loop concept to education, we quickly observe how inadequate and incomplete our data infrastructure is. We are unable to close the loop and connect data sets across education to and through the workforce. Economist Anthony Carnevale explains, "In spite of its growing economic importance, our postsecondary education and training system and labor market information systems remain disconnected. . . . [P]roviding information systems linking postsecondary education and training programs with career pathways is desperately needed."[5]

Connecting the Data

To connect the silos of K–12 learning, postsecondary education, and workforce development, we must aspire to the same sort of dense network of connections that leads to greater intelligence. The problem is not a dearth of data. Take the simple, or not so simple, act of choosing where to go to college. There is a wealth of information available, from state-wide data systems to the Department of Education's College Scorecard, as well as unemployment insurance data on wage earnings—all with the potential to provide education consumers a clearer view of programs and their enrollment and employment outcomes.

But few of these systems are easily comprehensible, and many data sets are closed off from public view. Federal law currently prevents students and families from finding the sort of outcomes information that might enable them to make better decisions about where to go to school. Very little data exists beyond *U.S. News & World Report's* rankings to help students and families make sense of what is usually one of the largest investments of their lives. For more mature adult learners, the resources are even scarcer.

We do not have a network of signals moving imperceptibly from one silo to another because data sets today are scattered, segregated, and unintegrated. Although many large employers, such as Walmart, Amazon, and AT&T, are tackling skills gap issues internally, they are not sharing or distributing their learnings more broadly; each is forging ahead with its own idiosyncratic and silo-specific initiatives. The lack of a robust data infrastructure also forecloses the opportunity for more ecosystem stakeholders to collaborate and share data.

There are glimmers of hope from alliances such as Massachusetts Commonwealth Corporation, San Diego Workforce Partnerships, Skills for Chicagoland's Future, and the Georgia Department of Economic Development. The Greater Houston Partnership is particularly ambitious in convening 100 of the various ecosystem stakeholders to develop a new talent pipeline of 500,000 workers. Unfortunately, such intra- or multi-industry collaborations are rare. Companies and organizations have a hard time setting aside their competitive lens of the market in service of a common agenda, and coalition building can quickly devolve into a game of herding cats.

One major stumbling block is that even when groups seek to behave differently and coordinate more effectively, there is a lack of real-time, accurate, and relevant information. Data are fragmented, hard to find, of varying levels of quality, and often locked away in government or proprietary sources or the black box of AI. The absence of reliable, connected, and widely available data creates more friction between all actors in the ecosystem. Stakeholders lack a common fact base or common set of data to refer to in pulling together a shared understanding of skills, good jobs, and upward mobility.

We cannot continue to muddle our way through in this way. Working learners need clear information to help them navigate education and career opportunities. The only way to connect navigation with comprehensive advising support, better funding options, targeted, relevant, and timely education, and transparent hiring is to fill in our information gaps and integrate data better. A more robust and open data infrastructure is a critical component to unlocking better insights and approaching that "near intelligence" of a natural root system.

Growing the Roots of a New Learning Ecosystem

Matt Gee is the cofounder and CEO of BrightHive as well as a senior research fellow at the Center for Data Science and Public Policy at the University of Chicago. His company is working on the data infrastructure "plumbing" to create better intelligence in the talent marketplace.

BrightHive is a data technology company that uses data trusts to help organizations, networks, and communities securely and responsibly link their data to empower individual and collective decision making and send clearer signals about in-demand jobs and skills to educational organizations and job seekers. BrightHive is actively working to help shape the future of work through its collaborations with employers, state and federal agencies, and nonprofits.

The fundamental barrier to building a better way forward became very clear to Gee in 2013 after seeing the same recurring challenges around data. He committed his life's work to "making data work for people": "I want to solve that problem at the most fundamental area in a way that it's going to scale the most and have the broadest impact. And if over and over again the problem was data sharing, data sharing, data sharing, then I wanted to find a replicable, scalable, cheap, and technology-enabled way to do that that was ethical and responsible—that didn't just replicate the existing, extractive, business models of our current data economy, but really put the power and control back into the hands of the institutions and the people that ultimately represented in this data."[6] In order to improve communication between multiple stakeholder groups, BrightHive is building "data trusts" for the talent marketplace. Gee explains the concept of a data trust as "a unified legal, technical, and governance framework that allows for networks of organizations to be able to combine their data ethically and responsibly to achieve a shared goal or a shared mission."[7] At their core, data trusts enable institutions' data to talk to one another.

All of this work, which Gee jokingly deems "unsexy," encompasses issues such as data sharing agreements, data standards, interoperability, and what is called ETL, or extraction, transmission, and loading. This is the hard work of making three very different languages speak to one another: the languages of employers, education training providers, and job seekers—all of which are completely different. He elaborates:

> In a lot of states, there is a strong desire to be able to know whether education and training programs are worth the money you are paying for them. What's the return on investment to education? It turns out answering that question is tricky. You need to figure out a way for individual student records that have an important set of considerations in their use and are managed and stewarded over by sometimes private institutions, sometimes public institutions, or nonprofit organizations that are providing education and training, to be linked with other very sensitive and very private data that's held by maybe a state, a workforce agency, or unemployment insurance office. And that data says what kinds of wages people make as they go on and work in the labor market over the next several years.
>
> Those are two very sensitive, very important datasets that, historically, we've had a difficult time figuring out how to get them to talk to each other and connect—and do it in a way that complies with all the necessary laws, but more importantly, in a way that really honors the sacred trust that each of those institutions, the government institution on one side and the education training institution on the other side, have with the people that they serve.

We don't have a way of doing this that works, so we just won't do it at all. And what that ends up creating for the talent marketplace is a complete lack of information about whether or not we actually are seeing meaningful returns to different kinds of credentials from different kinds of providers. And that prevents us from being able to compare apples to apples, and even being able to distinguish apples from oranges. . . .

We have so much data out there in education systems and so much data in HR information systems, and yet we have a fundamental disconnect between education and work. We have an increasingly disconnected learning market system that's driving social inequality. And we aren't using this increasingly valuable asset—our own data—to try to increase an opportunity for every individual in this country.[8]

Gee explains that despite these challenges, we are now finally able to connect the three languages and turn this challenge into a "Rosetta Stone moment."

BrightHive's platform does not replace the data infrastructure of groups but instead adds the connective tissue needed to connect networks and siloes to diverse technology stacks, different customer relation management systems, and different databases that are already in place. Gee explains that the key is to layer the data platform on top of existing infrastructure and connect the piping to make "sure you've got the right kind of ethical and security monitors on those pipes."

Data trusts link together various data sets while ensuring that groups retain control over all of their data. Two fundamental organizing principles of data trusts created by BrightHive are self-sovereignty and transparency. BrightHive does not become the owner of these pools of data; the members of the trust maintain that control.

As an example, in the state of Colorado, the departments of K–12, higher education, labor and employment as well as the state's workforce agency have formed a data trust as a multiagency group.

They seek to build a responsible and ethical way of linking the right kinds of data to help with career navigation and college navigation for their constituents.

In the state of Virginia, several government agencies are creating a data trust so that they can better coordinate referrals across higher education, workforce, and health and human services. In this way, the data trust can follow a single individual across several agencies.

The nonprofit Goodwill Industries International is using a data trust to coordinate its 157 local member organizations spread across the country to measure the outcomes of their education and training programs. The data trust is enabling Goodwill to track the future wage and employment outcomes for the people whom they serve.

Data trusts also work for public-private partnerships. BrightHive is also working with the Chamber of Commerce Foundation on the Jobs Data Exchange, an employer-side trust. Because there is no standardization in how job seekers write their resumes and employers post job openings, the result is what Gee calls the "garbage in, garbage out" problem.

In an attempt to rectify the situation, BrightHive and the Chamber are convening regular sessions with ADP Workforce Now, SAP SuccessFactors, and major employers to create a common competency model. The technological enabler will be an application programming interface for the creation of job postings, which will lead to more structured data linking skills and competencies. Starting with a minimum viable coalition of employers such as IBM and Toyota, these groups are trying to increase the signal quality between employers and job seekers.

Each of these initiatives is emblematic of the complex work needed to link and mobilize employers, policymakers, funders, and education and training providers around a shared language and agenda to serve more working learners. Ultimately, we are going to need to see more solutions that serve as this kind of interstitial tissue, pulling together multiple, static, disconnected data sets into one root system.

A more robust data infrastructure will be the foundation for any new learning ecosystem. If we can begin to close the loop of data, we will be able to engage in better guidance, preparation, funding, endorsement, and signal matching for all working learners. And we'll also rest assured that the next job transition that we face, as well as the 15 or 20 after that, will feel more easily navigable, supported, targeted, integrated, and transparent—no matter how uncertain the future of work may be.

CONCLUSION

Work is important not only for people's economic success but also for its ability to provide purpose and meaning, self-respect and dignity; work builds communities and allows individuals to contribute to the larger well-being of society. Every American should have the opportunity and resources needed to prepare for and pursue work that offers them a fair chance at both economic security and meaningful contributions to society. The United States should dedicate itself urgently to rebuilding the links among work, opportunity, and economic security for Americans.

—Council on Foreign Relations[1]

The robots are coming . . . sort of.

One puzzling aspect of the macroeconomic growth in this country is what MIT economist Daron Acemoglu calls "'so-so' automation," or technologies that are not sufficiently productive to displace workers fully and create new and more creative forms of labor that benefit people.[2]

Acemoglu points out that we are not witnessing the same sorts of countervailing effects that were generated when ATMs were first developed, for example. As ATMs began to proliferate, the role of bank tellers did not disappear. But it was precisely because ATMs worked so well at displacing human tellers from the routine task of doling out money that these machines also created the demand for a more extensive line of services in customer service, retention, and personalized advising for business banking or mortgage services in which humans held a comparative advantage. Concurrently, the banking industry matched that demand with talent and skills development, facilitating that entire adjustment process.

The same phenomenon is not occurring each time we introduce a new robot or new form of artificial intelligence into the world. To illustrate, even with the more than 100,000 robots that power Amazon's warehouse fulfillment centers, the retail giant is still heavily reliant on its 600,000 warehouse workers.[3] Warehouse automation is a "so-so" technology because roboticists have yet to figure out how to train a robot to grasp an object and adjust its grip. (This is astonishing when we consider that most infants learn how to do this as soon as they begin to grasp an adult's fingertip or hold a bottle.)

As a result, Amazon relies on hundreds of thousands of humans to intuit, recognize, pick, and pack products. "There is at present no cost-effective robotic facsimile for these human pickers," explains David Autor, another MIT economist. "The job's steep requirements for flexibility, object recognition, physical dexterity and fine motor coordination are too formidable."[4]

Are These the Jobs of the Future?

Although these tasks involve perception, manipulation, dexterity, and physical adaptability—skills that sound impressive—the work is hardly creative or rewarding. Indeed, with the dramatic increase in online shopping, human pickers are forced to engage in backbreaking work at high speeds.

In his investigative reporting, HBO host John Oliver revealed that Amazon workers can walk up to 15 miles or more per day in the warehouses, and "the injury and illness rate in the warehouse industry is higher than industries like coal mining, construction and logging."[5]

In October 2018, *The New York Times* reported that as many as six different women had miscarriages from lifting boxes weighing up to 45 pounds for XPO, a logistics company that has worked with

Amazon.[6] These women had been denied breaks because of intensified pressure to get as many as 120 boxes out per hour—up from 60 boxes per hour.

In the summers, workers toil in facilities that lack air conditioning, where temperatures rise as high as 100 degrees. A 58-year-old woman died of cardiac arrest in October 2017 after requesting time to rest because she felt ill. After she collapsed and died, employees were ordered to work around her body to keep pace with the grueling schedule.[7]

These stories obviously paint the worst portrait of stultifying, dead-end jobs. Nevertheless, we must ask: Are these the jobs of the future? Because some of these new jobs are truly worrisome.

Another work example comes from Amazon's Mechanical Turk, which facilitates the work of 500,000 "Turkers" worldwide working on "human intelligence tasks."[8] These activities include cleaning up data and training AI for language-recognition and machine-learning applications. This may sound like lofty work, but it's all for pennies on the dollar. Turkers take care of tasks that are broken down into something that can be accomplished in a matter of seconds or minutes. These tasks include tagging photos—making sure that thing is not a penis or child porn—transcribing podcasts, or entering data.

Mary Gray and Siddharth Suri illuminate this hidden world of micro- or crowd work in their book, *Ghost Work*:

> Billions of people consume website content, search engine queries, tweets, posts, and mobile-app-enabled services every day. They assume that their purchases are made possible by the magic of technology alone. But, in reality, they are being served by an international staff, quietly laboring in the background. These jobs, dominated by freelance and contingent work arrangements rather than full-time or even hourly wage positions, have no established, legal status.[9]

This quiet laboring is not necessarily stimulating, fulfilling, or steady work. Without powerful enough productivity effects, we need more people—more ghosts—to fill the interstitial space between robot and human.

The Future Only We Can Write

We do not have to succumb to the present of work—to what we have today. But we cannot sit still and hope that things won't change too much. The exponential future we face will not simply let up—nor can we will it to do so. If we simply admire the problem or try to resist or curb advancements, we will see innovations burgeon in other pockets instead.

Futurists at Singularity University point to Americans' discomfort with gene editing as an example.[10] American laws prohibit work on stem cells and gene research. None of that, however, has an impact on Chinese scientists who are moving full throttle on this kind of research. By opting out of innovation, we must wonder whether we are missing out on helping to steer potential, exponential transformations toward a better future. As futurist Brian David Johnson writes, "We build the future—the way to prepare for the future is to invent it. If we do not take action, we cede control, turning the future over to others—or worse, to the mindless efficiencies of technology or economic greed."[11]

It takes significant effort to overcome our way of thinking, redirect our energies into more constructive mental models, and move toward action. But it is not impossible. Knowing the future that we don't want, we can better articulate the future that we do want and then build toward that.

But doing so involves investing now in designing a new ecosystem for long-life learning. It will be a massive lift, but we *can* build the future of learning and work. We can take the limiting factors of our current environment, identify those pain points as moments of vulnerability today, and then transform them for the sake of all of us who will need help in not just a single transition from education to work but in the innumerable transitions to come. We must recognize the immense frictions that arise as we navigate job transitions. They stem from both a lack of visibility of our education and career options as well as deep racial, geographic, and socioeconomic inequities.

A healthy future learning ecosystem will enable transparency and easily understood ways of paying for and integrating further education; it will offer human touch points, community, and guidance as well as access to targeted education and good jobs. It will engender more and fairer opportunities for people to find creative forms of work as well as that sense of pride and self-worth.

Work provides more than money. People talk about the "dignity of work" to capture the sense of purpose and empowerment derived from making a contribution to society. The story about the future of learning and work is the story we tell ourselves—the one that only we can write. In order to bring a more equitable vision of the future into being, we must start behaving differently today. We must cocreate and knit together solutions that bridge the opportunity gap for job seekers who are furthest removed from generating wealth, power, and mobility.

The future of work that we thought we could worry about five or 10 years later is here and now. By centering on the future of workers, we smooth the way not only for the more than 41 million Americans being left behind today, but also for the entire workforce—for all of us—to embrace our new imperative for long-life learning and earning.

It's time to build.

ENDNOTES

Introduction

1. Michelle R. Weise and Clayton M. Christensen, *Hire Education: Mastery, Modularization, and the Workforce Revolution* (Redwood City, CA: Clayton Christensen Institute, 2014), https://www.christenseninstitute.org/wp-content/uploads/2014/07/Hire-Education.pdf.

2. Clayton M. Christensen, *The Innovator's Dilemma: When New Technologies Cause Great Firms to Fail* (Boston: Harvard Business School Press, 1997).

3. Estelle Sommeiller, Mark Price, and Ellis Wazeter, *Income Inequality in the U.S. by State, Metropolitan Area, and County* (Washington, DC: Economic Policy Institute, 2016), https://www.epi.org/publication/income-inequality-in-the-us.

4. Lance Lambert, "45.7 million have filed for unemployment during the pandemic–greater than the combined population of 23 states," Fortune, June 18, 2020, https://fortune.com/2020/06/18/45-7-million-have-filedunemployment-during-the-pandemic-greater-than-the-combined-population-of-23-states/.

5. Daniel Pink, "College Unbound Presents a Talk with Daniel Pink," May 1, 2020, Zoom, https://us02web.zoom.us/j/3518520288?pwd=SFpcMm5nclpM UW1QZDVCL1UxVUpUUT09.

6. 41,432,159 people to be exact. Strada Institute analysis of U.S. Census Bureau, American Community Survey (ACS), One-Year Public Use Microdata Sample (PUMS), 2018; generated by John Ratte using data.census.gov, https://www2 .census.gov/programs-surveys/acs/data/pums/2018/1-Year/.

Chapter 1

1. Lynda Gratton and Andrew Scott, *The 100-Year Life: Living and Working in an Age of Longevity* (London: Bloomsbury Information, 2016), 16.

2. Johannes Koettl, *The Physiological Limits of Life: Will Humans One Day Live to the Age of 150 Years?* (Washington, DC: Brookings, December 14, 2015), https://www.brookings.edu/blog/future-development/2015/12/14/the-physiological-limits-of-life-will-humans-one-day-live-to-the-age-of-150-years.

3. Linda Poon, "How Should We Prepare for a Rapidly Aging Global Population?" CityLab, September 8, 2015, https://www.citylab.com/equity/2015/09/what-a-rapidly-aging-global-population-means-for-the-world/403051/.

4. There's even something called *ammortality*, arguably the next big and sexy market opportunity. It's a term that investment analysts use to describe the market of innovations in delaying death. Some view it as one of the most lucrative investment opportunities of the future. Bank of America Merrill Lynch analysts expect the market of ammortality, which includes genomics, big data, and wellness, to be worth at least $600 billion. Thomas Franck, "Human Lifespan Could Soon Pass 100 Years Thanks to Medical Tech, Says BofA," *CNBC*, May 8, 2019, https://www.cnbc.com/2019/05/08/techs-next-big-disruption-could-be-delaying-death.html;

Ammortality is just one instantiation of a myriad of projections out there that scientific and technological advancements are soon going to be able to prolong life well beyond 100 years. David Sinclair is an Australian geneticist and professor at Harvard Medical School who is attempting to stop the aging process. He believes that "it will be possible one day to be immortal." Derek Thompson, "Can We Extend Human Lifespans to 150?" *Crazy/Genius*, Podcast audio, September 13, 2018;

Sinclair describes the aging process with this metaphor: "[I]f DNA is the digital information on a compact disc, then aging is due to scratches. We are searching for the polish." "The Sinclair Lab Research," Harvard Medical School, https://genetics.med.harvard.edu/sinclair/research.php; That polish, as he describes it, consists of the molecules that stop the decline of nicotinamide adenine dinucleotide (NAD+) levels in our bodies.

Sinclair believes that he is very much onto a way of increasing the body's creation of NAD+. He knows because he has been using his own body as a testing site. When he was 47, he took a test to measure his biomarkers. At that time, he had the biological profile of someone who was 58 years old. For three months, he regularly ingested a few molecules— resveratrol and something called SRT1720—to increase mitochondrial function. The next time he measured biomarkers, the age of his DNA reflected that of someone who was 31.4 years old. He has been taking a few molecules for the last ten years, as has his wife, his brother, and his 70-year-old father. His father testifies that the pain in his extremities has gone away and his energy has rebounded; he no longer groans when he gets out of bed. Assured that the method is working, Sinclair concludes, "I don't see any reason why a child that's born today couldn't make it to 150." Derek Thompson, "Can Science Cure Aging?" *The Atlantic*, September 13, 2018, https://www.theatlantic.com/ideas/archive/2018/09/can-science-cure-aging/570121.

5. Craig Copeland, "Labor Force Participation Rates by Age and Gender and the Age and Gender Composition of the U.S. Civilian Labor Force and Adult Population," *EBRI Issue Brief*, no. 449, May 18, 2018, https://www.ebri.org/docs/default-source/ebri-issue-brief/ebri_ib_449_lfp-8may18.pdf.

6. Paul Taylor, *The Next America* (Washington: DC, Pew Research, 2014), https://www.pewresearch.org/next-america/#Who-Are-the-Millennials.

7. Bureau of Labor Statistics, "Number of Jobs, Labor Market Experience, and Earnings Growth Among Americans at 50," Economic News Release, August 24, 2017, https://www.bls.gov/news.release/archives/nlsoy_08242017.htm.

8. Out of the $246 billion the federal government issues in student aid, the lion's share goes to those enrolled in undergraduate degree programs. "In 2018–19, undergraduate students received 76% ($186.9 billion) of total student aid, including 96% of all federal grants and 58% of federal loans. They received 86% of total grant aid from all sources and 62% of all loans, including nonfederal loans. The remainder of the aid funded graduate students." Sandy Baum, Jennifer Ma, Matea Pender, and C. J. Libassi, *Trends in Student Aid 2019* (New York: College Board, 2019), https://research.collegeboard.org/pdf/trends-student-aid-2019-full-report .pdf.

9. Sohan Murthy, "Top 10 Job Titles That Didn't Exist 5 Years Ago [Info-graphic]," LinkedIn Talent Blog, LinkedIn, January 6, 2014, https://business .linkedin.com/talent-solutions/blog/2014/01/top-10-job-titles-that-didnt-exist-5-years-ago-infographic.

10. Bureau of Labor Statistics, "69.7 Percent of 2016 High School Graduates Enrolled in College in October 2016," *TED: The Economics Daily*, U.S. Department of Labor, May 22, 2017, https://www.bls.gov/opub/ted/2017/69-point-7-percent-of-2016-high-school-graduates-enrolled-in-college-in-october-2016.htm?view_full; not all, of course, complete their college educations.

11. Christina Chang Wei and Laura Horn, "Federal Student Loan Debt Burden of Noncompleters," Institute of Education Sciences, U.S. Department of Education, April 2013, https://nces.ed.gov/pubs2013/2013155.pdf.

12. Doug Shapiro et al., *Some College No Degree: A National View of Students with Some College Enrollment, but No Completion* (Herndon, VA: National Student Clearinghouse Research Center, 2014), https://nscresearchcenter.org/wp-content/uploads/NSC_Signature_Report_7.pdf.

13. Kevin Kelly, *The Inevitable: Understanding the 12 Technological Forces That Will Shape Our Future* (New York: Viking Press, 2016).

14. David Autor, "Polanyi's Paradox and the Shape of Employment Growth," NBER Working Paper no. 20485, September 2014, doi:10.3386/w20485.

15. Michael Polanyi, *The Tacit Dimension* (Chicago: University of Chicago Press, 2009).

16. James Manyika et al., *A Future That Works: Automation, Employment, and Productivity* (New York: McKinsey Global Institute, 2017), https://www.mckinsey.com/featured-insights/digital-disruption/harnessing-automation-for-a-future-that-works.

17. The World Economic Forum similarly categorizes our uniquely human skills as coordinating with others, emotional intelligence, negotiation, persuasion, service orientation, training, and teaching others. World Economic Forum Centre for the New Economy and Society, *The Future of Jobs Report 2018* (Geneva: World Economic Forum, 2018), http://www3.weforum.org/docs/WEF_Future_of_Jobs_2018.pdf.

18. In a Brookings report on automation and AI, the authors classify computers and robots as being much less adept than humans at "creative intelligence (ideation, critical thinking, problem solving)" and "social intelligence (intuition, teamwork, persuasion, situational adaptability, perceptiveness, caring for others)." Mark Muro, Robert Maxim, and Jacob Whiton, "Automation and Artificial Intelligence: How Machines Are Affecting People and Places," Brookings, January 24, 2019, https://www.brookings.edu/research/automation-and-artificial-intelligence-how-machines-affect-people-and-places.

19. Michelle R. Weise, Andrew Hanson, Rob Sentz, and Yustina Saleh, *Robot-Ready: Human+ Skills for the Future of Work* (Indianapolis, IN: Strada Institute for the Future of Work, 2019), https://www.stradaeducation.org/report/robot-ready/.

20. Geoff Colvin, *Humans Are Underrated: What High Achievers Know That Brilliant Machines Never Will* (New York: Portfolio, 2015).

21. Colvin, *Humans Are Underrated*, 26.

22. Colvin, *Humans Are Underrated*, 57.

23. Eli Pariser, "Beware Online 'Filter Bubbles,'" TED video, 8:49, March 2011, https://www.ted.com/talks/eli_pariser_beware_online_filter_bubbles.

24. Josh Bersin, "Google for Jobs: Disrupting the Gigantic Recruiting Market?" *LinkedIn Pulse*, May 25, 2017, https://www.linkedin.com/pulse/google-jobs-disrupting-gigantic-recruiting-market-josh-bersin.

25. Northeastern University president Joseph Aoun has devoted an entire book to the concept of "humanics": "a new model of learning that enables learners to understand the highly technological world around them and that simultaneously allows them to transcend it by nurturing the mental and intellectual qualities that are unique to humans—namely their capacity for creativity and mental flexibility." Joseph Aoun, *Robot-Proof: Higher Education in the Age of Artificial Intelligence* (Cambridge, MA: MIT Press, 2018), 53.

26. Jim Collins and Jerry Porras, *Built to Last: Successful Habits of Visionary Companies* (New York: Harper Business, 1997).

27. Scott Hartley, *The Fuzzy and the Techie: Why the Liberal Arts Will Rule the Digital World* (New York: Houghton Mifflin Harcourt, 2017).

28. Lee Rainie, "Technological Innovation? That's the Easy Part," in *TREND: Analysis of the Facts, Numbers, and Trends Shaping the World*, Summer 2017, Pew Charitable Trusts, https://www.pewtrusts.org/-/media/post-launch-images/trend-magazine/summer-2017/trend_summer_2017.pdf.

29. Quoted in Emily Chang, *Brotopia: Breaking Up the Boys' Club of Silicon Valley* (New York: Portfolio, 2018), 8.

30. Gregory Chan (Engineering Project Manager, Apple), interview with author, September 2016.

31. Tarmo Virki, "Finland Seeks to Teach 1% of All Europeans Basics on AI," Reuters, December 10, 2019, https://www.reuters.com/article/us-finland-education-ai/finland-seeks-to-teach-1-of-all-europeans-basics-on-ai-idUSKBN1YE1B6.

32. Paul Daugherty and H. James Wilson, *Human + Machine: Reimagining Work in the Age of AI* (Boston: Harvard Business Review Press, 2018), 129.

33. Shana Lynch, "Andrew Ng: Why AI Is the New Electricity," *Stanford Business*, March 11, 2017, https://www.gsb.stanford.edu/insights/andrew-ng-why-ai-new-electricity

34. Stephen Hawking, "Opening Night of #WebSummit 2017," Presentation at #WebSummit 2017, Lisbon, Portugal, November 6, 2017.

35. "Open Loop University," Stanford 2025, accessed May 8, 2020, http://www
    .stanford2025.com/open-loop-university.

36. Michael Barber, Katelyn Donnelly, and Saad Rizvi, "An Avalanche Is Com-
    ing: Higher Education and the Revolution Ahead," Institute for Public Policy
    Research, March 2013, https://www.ippr.org/publications/an-avalanche-is-
    coming-higher-education-and-the-revolution-ahead.

37. Quoted in Kellie Woodhouse, "Arts and Sciences Deficits," *Inside Higher Ed*,
    June 4, 2015, https://www.insidehighered.com/news/2015/06/04/colleges-
    arts-and-sciences-struggle-deficits-enrollment-declines.

38. George McCully, "Pushing Back on Higher Education as Trainer for
    High-Tech Jobs," New England Board of Higher Education, June 21, 2016,
    https://nebhe.org/journal/pushing-back-on-higher-education-as-trainer-for-
    high-tech-jobs.

39. McCully, "Pushing Back."

40. American Academy of Arts and Sciences, *The Future of Undergraduate Edu-
    cation, The Future of America* (Cambridge, MA: Author, 2017), https://www
    .amacad.org/publication/future-undergraduate-education.

41. Quoted in Samuel M. Hines Jr., *Creating the Entrepreneurial University to Sup-
    port Liberal Education* (Washington, DC: American Association of Colleges
    and Universities, 2008), 29–30.

42. Ben Wildavsky, Andrew Hanson, and Tony Carnevale, "Season 2, Episode
    1: Tony Carnevale," April 22, 2020, in *Lessons Earned Podcast*, produced by
    Strada Education Network, https://www.stradaeducation.org/podcast/episode-
    1-tony-carnevale/.

43. Ellen Bara Stolzenberg et al., *The American Freshman: National Norms Fall
    2018* (Los Angeles: Higher Education Research Institute, UCLA, 2019),
    https://www.heri.ucla.edu/monographs/TheAmericanFreshman2018.pdf;
    "CIRP Freshman Survey," UCLA Higher Education Research Institute,
    https://heri.ucla.edu/cirp-freshman-survey.

44. Data were first presented here when only 86,000 responses had come
    in: https://www.stradaeducation.org/report/why-higher-ed/. These new
    percentages have been calculated based on all 350,000 survey responses being
    tallied.

45. Strada Center for Consumer Insights, "COVID-19 Work and Education Sur-
    vey: Week 5 Results," Public Viewpoint, Strada Education Network, April
    2020, https://www.stradaeducation.org/wp-content/uploads/2020/04/Public-
    Viewpoint-Report-Week-5.pdf.

46. Strada Education Network and Gallup. *2017 College Student Survey: A Nationally Representative Survey of Currently Enrolled Students*, January 17, 2018, https://www.stradaeducation.org/report/crisis-of-confidence-current-college-students-do-not-feel-prepared-for-the-workforce/.

47. Wildavsky et al., "Season 2, Episode 1: Tony Carnevale," *Lessons Earned Podcast.*

48. All statistics in this section come from Burning Glass Technologies and Strada Institute for the Future of Work, "The Permanent Detour: Underemployment's Long-Term Effects on the Careers of College Grads," May 2018, https://www.burning-glass.com/wp-content/uploads/permanent_detour_underemployment_report.pdf.

Chapter 2

1. Jennifer Ma, Sandy Baum, Matea Pender, and CJ Libassi, "Trends in College Pricing 2019," College Board, November 2019, https://research.collegeboard.org/pdf/trends-college-pricing-2019-full-report.pdf.

2. Board of Governors of the Federal Reserve System (US), "Student Loans Owned and Securitized, Outstanding [SLOAS]," retrieved from FRED, Federal Reserve Bank of St. Louis, accessed November 5, 2019, https://fred.stlouisfed.org/series/SLOAS.

3. National Center for Education Statistics, "Table 317.10. Degree-Granting Postsecondary Institutions, by Control and Level of Institution: Selected Years, 1949–50 through 2017–18," *Digest of Education Statistics*, U.S. Department of Education, December 2019, https://nces.ed.gov/programs/digest/d18/tables/dt18_317.10.asp.

4. National Center for Education Statistics, "Table 303.10. Total Fall Enrollment in Degree-Granting Postsecondary Institutions, by Attendance Status, Sex of Student, and Control of Institution: Selected Years, 1947 through 2028," *Digest of Education Statistics*, U.S. Department of Education, December 2019, https://nces.ed.gov/programs/digest/d18/tables/dt18_303.10.asp.

5. National Center for Education Statistics, "Table 317.10."

6. Exact statistic is 69.7 percent of 2016 high school graduates; not all, of course, complete their college educations. Bureau of Labor Statistics, "69.7 Percent of 2016 High School Graduates Enrolled in College in October 2016," *TED: The Economics Daily*, May 22, 2017, https://www.bls.gov/opub/ted/2017/69-point-7-percent-of-2016-high-school-graduates-enrolled-in-college-in-october-2016.htm?view_full

7. Peace Bransberger and Demaree Michelau, *Knocking at the College Door: Executive Summary* (Boulder, CO: Western Interstate Commission for Higher Education, 2016), https://knocking.wiche.edu/reports/2017/3/22/full-report.

8. Nathan Grawe, "The Enrollment Crash Goes Deeper than Demographics," *The Chronicle Review*, November 1, 2019, https://www.chronicle.com/interactives/20191101-Grawe.

9. Seth Reynolds et al., "Strength in Numbers: Strategies for Collaborating in a New Era for Higher Education," Parthenon-EY Education Practice, 2016, https://cdn.ey.com/parthenon/pdf/perspectives/P-EY_Strength-in-Numbers-Collaboration-Strategies_Paper_Final_082016.pdf.

10. National Center for Education Statistics, "Table 317.10."

11. Anemona Hartocollis, "After Coronavirus, Colleges Worry: Will Students Come Back?" *The New York Times*, April 15, 2020, https://www.nytimes.com/2020/04/15/us/coronavirus-colleges-universities-admissions.html.

12. Latest data available at the time of writing this book is from 2017. National Center for Education Statistics, U.S. Department of Education, "Table 303.40: Total Fall Enrollment in Degree-Granting Postsecondary Institutions, by Attendance Status, Sex, and Age: Selected Years, 1970 through 2028," *Digest of Education Statistics*, March 2019, https://nces.ed.gov/programs/digest/d18/tables/dt18_303.40.asp.

13. U.S. Census Bureau, "Table S2602: Characteristics of the Group Quarters Population by Group Quarters Type (3 Types)," 2017 American Community Survey, https://data.census.gov/cedsci/table?q=S2602&tid=ACSST1Y2018.S2602.

14. National Center for Education Statistics, "Table 303.10."

15. National Center for Education Statistics, U.S. Department of Education, "Table 303.40."

16. Quoted in Kevin Carey, *The End of College: Creating the Future of Learning and the University of Everywhere* (New York: Riverhead Books, 2016), 180.

17. Carey, *The End of College*, 51.

18. Clayton M. Christensen, *The Innovator's Dilemma: When New Technologies Cause Great Firms to Fail* (Boston: Harvard Business School Press, 1997).

19. National Center for Education Statistics, "Table 303.20: Total Fall Enrollment in All Postsecondary Institutions Participating in Title IV Programs and Annual Percentage Change in Enrollment, by Degree-Granting Status and Control of Institution: 1995 through 2017," *Digest of Education Statistics*, December 2019, https://nces.ed.gov/programs/digest/d18/tables/

dt18_303.20.asp; U.S. Senate Committee on Health, Education, Labor & Pensions, "Harkin: Report Reveals Troubling Realities for For-Profit Schools," Ranking Member's Newsroom, July 30, 2012, https://www.help.senate.gov/ranking/newsroom/press/harkin-report-reveals-troubling-realities-of-for-profit-schools; National Center for Education Statistics, "Table 303.10."

20. U.S. Senate Committee on Health, Education, Labor & Pensions, "Harkin: Report."

21. Brian Jacob, Brian McCall, and Kevin Stange, "College as Country Club: Do Colleges Cater to Students' Preferences for Consumption?" NBER Working Paper No. 18745, January 2013, https://www.nber.org/papers/w18745.

22. Gordon C. Winston, "The Positional Arms Race in Higher Education," Williams Project on the Economics of Higher Education, Department of Economics, Williams College, 2000, https://ideas.repec.org/p/wil/wilehe/54.html.

23. Andrew S. Rosen, *Change.edu: Rebooting for the New Talent Economy* (New York: Kaplan Publishing, 2011), 1.

24. Phil Regier (CEO, EdPlus at ASU), interview with author, January 14, 2020.

25. While the starting point in the creation of a business model is the value proposition, once a business model has coalesced to deliver that value proposition, the causality of events begins to work in reverse, and the only value propositions that the organization can successfully take to market are those that fit the existing resources, processes, and profit formula.

26. A formula emerges as the company follows these processes to use its resources to deliver the value proposition. The revenue formula defines how large the organization must become to break even, what kind of gross and net margins it must achieve to cover the cost of its resources, and how rapidly it needs to turn its assets over to achieve an adequate return on investment. The revenue formula in turn determines the kinds of value propositions that the business model can and cannot offer. These four elements of the business model become interdependently locked very quickly. Innovations that conform to the business model are readily funded. Organizations sometimes reject an innovation that emerges to address a new need in the market but doesn't fit these four elements of the business model. But the organization more frequently co-opts such innovations by forcing them to conform to the business model in order to get funded. When this happens—funding only flows to innovations that sustain or fit the business model—the organization loses its ability to respond to fundamental changes in the markets that it serves. This is what has happened to many universities.

Another way to capture the incompatibility of a disruptive innovation within the business model of an established university is to consider the forces that encumber the legislative process. Even if a member of Congress were to identify and envision an innovative solution to a pressing societal problem, the introduction of a bill can evoke opposition from different constituencies, such as labor unions, chambers of commerce, or a powerful senator threatening to block the legislation—all of whom must be appeased in some way. As a result, in order to garner enough votes to be enshrined as law, the bill is modified to address the concerns and fit the interests of those with powerful votes. The result is a final bill that only faintly resembles the original innovative solution.

27. Thanks to Øystein Fjeldstad of the Norwegian School of Management, friend of the Christensen Institute, who developed and taught us this framework. For more information on Fjeldstad's framework, please refer to Charles B. Stabell and Øystein D. Fjeldstad, "Configuring Value for Competitive Advantage: On Chains, Shops and Networks," *Strategic Management Journal* 19 (1998): 413–437, https://onlinelibrary.wiley.com/doi/abs/10.1002/(SICI)1097-0266(199805)19:5%3C413::AID-SMJ946%3E3.0.CO;2-C.

28. Clayton M. Christensen and Michael Raynor, *The Innovator's Solution: Creating and Sustaining Successful Growth* (Boston: Harvard Business Review Press, 2013).

29. Christensen and Raynor, *The Innovator's Solution*, 127.

30. Quoted in Michelle R. Weise, "You Gotta Keep 'em Separated: How to Give CBE Breathing Room," *Competency Works*, January 21, 2015, https://www.competencyworks.org/higher-education-2/you-gotta-keep-em-separated-how-to-give-cbe-breathing-room.

31. Scott Pulsipher (President, West Governors University), interview with author, November 12, 2019.

32. Goldie Blumenstyk, "Meet the New Mega-University," *The Chronicle of Higher Education*, November 11, 2018, https://www.chronicle.com/article/Meet-the-New-Mega-University/245049.

33. In 2006, the U.S. Department of Education's Spellings Commission report proffered that accrediting agencies do little besides assessing inputs and processes as opposed to prioritizing student-learning outcomes. U.S. Department of Education, "A Test of Leadership: Charting the Future of U.S. Higher Education," A Report of the Commission Appointed by Secretary of Education Margaret Spelling, September 2006, http://www2.ed.gov/about/bdscomm/list/hiedfuture/reports/final-report.pdf.

34. Clayton M. Christensen, Michael B. Horn, and Curtis W. Johnson, *Disrupting Class: How Disruptive Innovation Will Change the Way the World Learns* (New York: McGraw-Hill, 2008).

35. Both Sony and Honda took advantage of disruptive distribution channels. Discount retailers such as Kmart, which had no after-sale capability to repair vacuum tube–based electronic products, were emerging at the same time as Sony's disruptive products. Solid-state radios and televisions constituted the fuel that enabled the discounters to disrupt appliance stores. By selecting a channel that had up-market disruptive potential itself, Sony harnessed the energies of that channel to promote and position its products. Honda's business took off when it began to distribute through power equipment and sporting goods retailers, because it gave those retailers a chance to migrate toward higher-margin product lines. In each of the most successful disruptions we have studied, the product and its channel to the customer formed this sort of mutually beneficial relationship.

36. Michelle R. Weise and Clayton M. Christensen, *Hire Education: Mastery, Modularization, and the Workforce Revolution* (San Mateo, CA: Clayton Christensen Institute for Disruptive Innovation, 2014), https://www.amazon .com/Hire-Education-Modularization-Workforce-Revolution-ebook/dp/ B00UUJYC46/ref=sr_1_1?dchild=1&keywords=%22hire+education%22& qid=1593810832&sr=8-1

37. Elena Silva, Taylor White, and Thomas Toch, *The Carnegie Unit: A Century-Old Standard in a Changing Education Landscape* (Stanford, CA: Carnegie Foundation for the Advancement of Teaching, 2015), https://www .carnegiefoundation.org/wp-content/uploads/2015/01/Carnegie_Unit_Report .pdf.

38. Paul Fain, "Keeping Up with Competency," *Inside Higher Ed*, September 10, 2015, https://www.insidehighered.com/news/2015/09/10/amid-competency- based-education-boom-meeting-help-colleges-do-it-right.

39. Massachusetts Institute of Technology, *Institute-Wide Task Force on the Future of MIT Education: Final Report*, July 2014, http://web.mit.edu/future-report/ TaskForceFinal_July28.pdf, 13.

40. Philip Trostel, *It's Not Just the Money: The Benefits of College Education to Individuals and to Society* (Indianapolis: Lumina Foundation, 2015), https://www .luminafoundation.org/files/resources/its-not-just-the-money.pdf. (Note: That's when you assume a discount rate of 3 percent. With no discount, it's $1.4 million for a BA or $2.5 million for an advanced degree, both relative to high school); U.S. Social Security Administration, "Education and Lifetime

Earnings," November 2015, https://www.ssa.gov/policy/docs/research-summaries/education-earnings.html; Anthony P. Carnevale, Stephen J. Rose, and Ban Cheah, *The College Payoff* (Washington, DC: Georgetown University Center on Education and the Workforce, 2011), https://cew.georgetown.edu/cew-reports/the-college-payoff; "How Can We Amplify Education as an Engine of Mobility?" *Opportunity Insights*, https://opportunityinsights.org/education.

41. Clark Gilbert (President, Brigham Young University–Pathway), interview with author, October 14, 2019.

42. Lilah Burke, "Who's Completing Microcredentials?" *Inside Higher Ed*, November 20, 2019, https://www.insidehighered.com/digital-learning/article/2019/11/20/new-report-offers-analysis-microcredential-completers.

43. Fiona Hollands and Aasiya Kazi, *Benefits and Costs of MOOC-Based Alternative Credentials: 2018–2019 Results from End-of-Program Surveys*, Center for Benefit-Cost Studies of Education, Columbia University Teachers College, November 2019, https://8606adb0-7829-4e6c-a502-3e181c6f3720.filesusr.com/ugd/cc7beb_a74e1be71afb4e72bb7f44adaf03d9eb.pdf.

44. Quoted in Burke, "Who's Completing Microcredentials?"

45. Lee Rainie and Janna Anderson, "The Future of Jobs and Jobs Training," Pew Research Center, May 3, 2017, https://www.pewresearch.org/internet/2017/05/03/the-future-of-jobs-and-jobs-training.

46. National Center for Education Statistics, "Table 326.20: Graduation Rate from First Institution Attended within 150 Percent of Normal Time for First-Time, Full-Time Degree/Certificate-Seeking Students at 2-Year Postsecondary Institutions, by Race/Ethnicity, Sex, and Control of Institution: Selected cohort Entry Years, 2000 through 2015," *Digest of Education Statistics*, 2019, U.S. Department of Education, https://nces.ed.gov/programs/digest/d19/tables/dt19_326.20.asp.

47. Laura Horn and Thomas Weko, "On Track to Complete? A Taxonomy of Beginning Community College Students and Their Outcomes 3 Years After Enrolling: 2003–04 through 2006," U.S. Department of Education, National Center for Education Statistics, July 28, 2009, http://nces.ed.gov/pubsearch/pubsinfo.asp?pubid=2009152.

48. Strada-Gallup Consumer Insights Survey Data, Education Consumer Pulse and Employer Surveys, 2018, https://www.stradaeducation.org/network/consumer-insights.

49. Northeastern University and Gallup, "Facing the Future: U.S., U.K. and Canadian Citizens Call for a Unified Skills Strategy for the AI Age," June 2019, https://www.northeastern.edu/gallup/pdf/Northeastern_Gallup_AI_2019.pdf.

50. Anthony P. Carnevale, Jeff Strohl, and Artem Gulish, *College Is Just the Beginning: Employers' Role in the $1.1 Trillion Postsecondary Education and Training System* (Washington, DC: Georgetown University Center on Education and the Workforce, 2015), https://cew.georgetown.edu/cew-reports/college-is-just-the-beginning/.

Chapter 3

1. Peter Cappelli, "Your Approach to Hiring Is All Wrong," *Harvard Business Review*, June 2019, https://hbr.org/2019/05/recruiting.

2. David Smith, Diego S. De León, Breck Marshall, and Susan M. Cantrell, "Solving the Skills Paradox: Seven Ways to Close Your Critical Skills Gaps," Accenture Institute for High Performance, 2012, https://youtheconomicopportunities.org/sites/default/files/uploads/resource/Accenture-Solving-the-Skills-Paradox.pdf.

3. Cappelli, "Your Approach to Hiring."

4. As MIT economist Erik Brynjolfsson explains: "Investing in new technology can often be easier for companies than negotiating the organizational challenges that come with reskilling workers." See Lauren Webber, "Why Companies Are Failing at Reskilling," *The Wall Street Journal*, April 19, 2019, https://www.wsj.com/articles/the-answer-to-your-companys-hiring-problem-might-be-right-under-your-nose-11555689542.

5. Michael E. Porter and Jan W. Rivkin, *An Economy Doing Half Its Job: Findings of Harvard Business School's 2013–14 Survey on U.S. Competitiveness* (Cambridge, MA: Harvard Business School, 2014), https://www.hbs.edu/competitiveness/documents/an-economy-doing-half-its-job.pdf.

6. Jake Schwartz, "The Costly Zero Sum Game That's Fueling the Skills Gap," *Forbes*, December 4, 2017, https://www.forbes.com/sites/realspin/2017/12/04/the-costly-zero-sum-game-thats-fueling-the-skills-gap/#77f218cd37d2.

7. PWC, "The Talent Challenge: Adapting to Growth," 17th Annual Global CEO Survey, October 2019, https://www.pwc.com/gx/en/services/people-organisation/publications/ceosurvey-talent-challenge.html.

8. According to the Bureau of Labor Statistics, "Overall employment of home
    health aides and personal care aides is projected to grow 36 percent from 2018
    to 2028, much faster than the average for all occupations." "Home Health
    Aides and Personal Care Aides," *Occupational Outlook Handbook*, U.S. Bureau
    of Labor Statistics, https://www.bls.gov/ooh/healthcare/home-health-aides-
    and-personal-care-aides.htm.

9. Joseph Fuller and Manjari Raman, "The Caring Company: How Employers
    Can Cut Costs and Boost Productivity by Helping Employees Manage Care-
    giving Needs," Harvard Business School, June 2019, https://www.hbs.edu/
    managing-the-future-of-work/Documents/The_Caring_Company.pdf.

10. Unless otherwise noted, all interviewee quotes are from Strada Institute for the
    Future of Work's research titled "Adult Learner Voices," conducted from Jan-
    uary 2019 to March 2020.

11. Paul Taylor and the Pew Research Center, *The Next America: Boomers, Mil-
    lennials, and the Looming Generational Showdown* (New York: Public Affairs,
    2014).

12. Taylor and Pew Research Center, *The Next America*.

13. Alicia H. Munnell, Matthew Rutledge, and Geoffrey Sanzenbacher, "Retiring
    Earlier Than Planned: What Matters Most?" no. 19–3, Center for Retirement
    Research at Boston College, February 2019, https://crr.bc.edu/wp-content/
    uploads/2019/01/IB_19-3.pdf.

14. U.S. Social Security Administration, *The 2019 Annual Report of the Board of
    Trustees of the Federal Old-Age and Survivors Insurance and Federal Disability
    Insurance Trust Funds*, April 22, 2019, https://www.ssa.gov/oact/TR/2019/
    tr2019.pdf; Alan Rappeport, "Social Security and Medicare Funds Face
    Insolvency, Report Finds," *The New York Times*, April 22, 2019, https://www
    .nytimes.com/2019/04/22/us/politics/social-security-medicare-insolvency
    .html.

15. OECD, "Overview: More and Better Opportunities to Work at an Older
    Age," *Working Better with Age*, https://www.oecd-ilibrary.org/employment/
    working-better-with-age_4426a1dc-en.

16. OECD, "Overview: More and Better Opportunities to Work at an Older
    Age."

17. Alicia H. Munnell, Steven Sass, and Mauricio Soto, "Employer Attitudes
    Towards Older Workers: Survey Results, Work Opportunities for Older
    Americans," *Center for Retirement Research at Boston College Issue Brief* 3, June
    2006, http://crr.bc.edu/wp-content/uploads/2006/07/wob_3.pdf; Also see

OECD, "Overview: More and Better Opportunities to Work at an Older Age," for a similar point.

18. Although age discrimination is difficult to prove, surveys in the European Union (2015), Australia (2015), the United States (2017), and Brazil (2018) indicate that a majority of respondents have witnessed or experienced it. Sixty percent of respondents to a European Union survey, including managers, stated that being over age 55 would disadvantage a job applicant relative to an equally qualified younger applicant. OECD, "Overview: More and Better Opportunities to Work at an Older Age."

19. David Neumark, Ian Burn, and Patrick Button, "Age Discrimination and Hiring of Older Workers," *FRBSF Economic Letter*, February 27, 2017, https://www.frbsf.org/economic-research/publications/economic-letter/2017/february/age-discrimination-and-hiring-older-workers.

20. There are technical reasons why it's hard to run this sort of study for mid- and high-skilled jobs. First, if a job requires ten years' experience in the field, it's unlikely that a 29- or 31-year-old would have ten years' experience. (Although one could compare people in their late 30s.) Second, the authors state that "labor economists . . . believe that realistic responses to fictitious job applicants are less likely in more high-skilled labor markets where employers are more likely to be familiar with job applicants."

21. Women applicants to administrative jobs aged 64–66 had a 7.6 percent callback rate compared to a 14.4 percent callback rate for identical applications from women aged 29–31. David Neumark, Ian Burn, and Patrick Button, "Is It Harder for Older Workers to Find Jobs? New and Improved Evidence from a Field Experiment," *Journal of Political Economy* 127, no. 2 (2019), 922–270, https://www.journals.uchicago.edu/doi/abs/10.1086/701029?journalCode=jpe&. A synopsis of the findings appears in Neumark, Burn, and Button, "Age Discrimination and Hiring of Older Workers."

22. Neumark, Burn, and Button, "Age Discrimination and Hiring of Older Workers."

23. OECD, "Overview: More and Better Opportunities to Work at an Older Age."

24. Biddle Consulting Group, "Uniform Guidelines on Employee Selection Procedures," http://www.uniformguidelines.com/uniformguidelines.html.

25. The Georgetown University Center on Education and the Workforce estimates that through 2020, the economy will create 24 million entirely new positions. Most of these jobs will be less physically intensive and emphasize skills

like active listening, leadership, communication, analytics, and management. Anthony P. Carnevale, Nicole Smith, and Jeff Strohl, *Recovery: Job Growth and Education Requirements Through 2020*, June 2013, https:// 1gyhoq479ufd3yna29x7ubjn-wpengine.netdna-ssl.com/wp-content/uploads/ 2014/11/Recovery2020.FR_.Web_.pdf; Joshua K. Hartstone and Laura T. Germine, "When Does Cognitive Functioning Peak? The Asynchronous Rise and Fall of Different Cognitive Abilities Across the Life Span," *Psychological Science* 26, no. 4 (2015): 433–443, https://d2dg4e62b1gc8m.cloudfront.net/ pub_pdfs/HartshorneGermine2015.pdf.

26. Marilyn Frye, *The Politics of Reality: Essays in Feminist Theory* (Berkeley, CA: Crossing Press, 1983), 4–5.

27. John Kania, Mark Kramer, and Peter Senge, *The Water of Systems Change*, FSG, May 2018, https://www.fsg.org/publications/water_of_systems_change.

28. William Gibson, "The Future Is Already Here—It's Just Not Evenly Distributed," *The Economist*, December 4, 2003.

29. Opportunity@Work, "Byron's Big Ideas: 'Three Points on the Future of Work,'" *Medium* (blog), October 11, 2018, https://blog.opportunityatwork .org/byrons-big-ideas-three-points-on-the-future-of-work-2cd6eccc7532.

30. 9.6 times more to be exact. OECD, "Improving job quality and reducing gender gaps are essential to tackling growing inequality," May 21, 2015, https:// www.oecd.org/social/reducing-gender-gaps-and-poor-job-quality-essential- to-tackle-growing-inequality.htm.

31. Edward Alden and Laura Taylor-Kale, *The Work Ahead: Machines, Skills, and US Leadership in the Twenty-First Century*, The Council on Foreign Relations, Independent Task Force Report no. 76, April 2018, https://www.cfr.org/ report/the-work-ahead/report.

32. Oren Cass, "America's Economy Is Both Booming—and Fading," *The Washington Post*, December 4, 2018, https://www.washingtonpost.com/ opinions/americas-economy-is-both-booming--and-fading/2018/12/04/ 758ca1bc-f7fe-11e8-8c9a-860ce2a8148f_story.html.

33. Strada Institute analysis of American Community Survey data, U.S. Census Bureau, 2018. For more information on the term "working class," please see Appendix 1A of Michelle Weise, Andrew Hanson, Allison Salisbury, and Kathy Qu, *On-ramps to Good Jobs: Fueling Innovation for the Learning Ecosystem of the Future*, Strada Institute for the Future of Work and Entangled Solutions, January 29, 2019, https://www.stradaeducation.org/report/on- ramps-to-good-jobs/. We use the term "working class" to refer to people who:

- Have less than an associate degree

- Are not earning a living wage. There is no consensus definition on what constitutes a living wage. We define a living wage as $35,000, as a more generous and inclusive benchmark associated with gainful employment among those established by the Department of Education, the Georgetown University Center on Education and the Workforce, and the Institute for Higher Education Policy.

- Have a family income of less than $70,000. The National Center for Children in Poverty estimates that American families need an income at least twice the federal poverty rate to cover their basic expenses. The cost of living varies across geographies, but $50,000 lies in the middle of the range for areas with high and low costs of living across the United States. Nancy K. Cauthen and Sarah Fass, "Measuring Poverty in the United States," National Center for Children in Poverty, 2008, http://www.nccp .org/publications/pub_825.html.

- We use $70,000 as a more generous measure of middle-class status to account for differences in the cost of living across the country. Our estimate relies on the U.S. Census Bureau's 2018 American Community Survey, a monthly cross-sectional survey of 250,000 households, or 3 million households each year. The American Community Survey includes information about respondents' educational attainment, earnings from employment, and family income.

34. Anthony Carnevale, Tamara Jayasundera, and Artem Gulish, *America's Divided Recovery: College Haves and Have-Nots* (Washington, DC: Georgetown University Center on Education and the Workforce, 2016), https:// 1gyhoq479ufd3yna29x7ubjn-wpengine.netdna-ssl.com/wp-content/uploads/ Americas-Divided-Recovery-web.pdf.

35. Pew Research Center, Social and Demographic Trends, "The Rising Cost of Not Going to College," February 11, 2014, https://www.pewsocialtrends.org/ 2014/02/11/the-rising-cost-of-not-going-to-college.

36. Raj Chetty, Nathaniel Hendren, Patrick Kline, and Emmanuel Saez, "Where Is the Land of Opportunity? The Geography of Intergenerational Mobility in the United States," National Bureau of Economic Research Working Paper 19843, 2014, https://www.nber.org/papers/w19843.pdf.

37. Strada Institute analysis of American Community Survey data, U.S. Census Bureau, 2018.

38. Oren Cass et al., *Works, Skills, Community: Restoring Opportunity for the Working Class*, Opportunity America, Brookings, and the American Enterprise Institute, 2018, http://opportunityamericaonline.org/wp-content/uploads/2018/10/WCG-final_web.pdf.

39. ProPublica and the Urban Institute have found that adults over 50 are commonly pushed into early retirement by employers. Richard W. Johnson and Peter Gosselin, *How Secure Is Employment at Older Ages?* (Washington, DC: Urban Institute, 2018), https://www.urban.org/research/publication/how-secure-employment-older-ages.

40. Discouraged workers, for example, include people who want and are available for work and who have looked for a job sometime in the prior 12 months. These adults are not counted as unemployed because they had not searched for work in the four weeks preceding the survey.

41. Anne Case and Angus Deaton, "Rising Morbidity and Mortality in Midlife among White Non-Hispanic Americans in the 21st Century," *PNAS* 112, no. 49 (December 8, 2018): 15078–15083, doi:10.1073/pnas.1518393112.

42. Anne Case and Angus Deaton, "Mortality and Morbidity in the 21st Century," Brookings Papers on Economic Activity, Spring 2017, https://www.brookings.edu/bpea-articles/mortality-and-morbidity-in-the-21st-century; David Leonhardt and Stuart A. Thompson, "How Working-Class Life Is Killing Americans, in Charts," *The New York Times*, March 6, 2020, https://www.nytimes.com/interactive/2020/03/06/opinion/working-class-death-rate.html.

43. Steven H. Woolf and Heidi Schoomaker, "Life Expectancy and Mortality Rates in the United States, 1959–2017," *JAMA* 322, no. 20 (November 26, 2019): 1996–2016, doi:10.1001/jama.2019.16932.

44. Doris Kearns Goodwin, *Team of Rivals* (New York: Simon & Schuster, 2005).

45. Matt Pearce, "'A Sea of Despair': White Americans without College Degrees Are Dying Younger," *The Los Angeles Times*, March 23, 2017, https://www.latimes.com/nation/la-na-white-health-20170323-story.html.

46. Quoted in Pearce, "'A Sea of Despair.'"

47. Quoted in Lauren Weber, "Why Companies Are Failing at Reskilling," *The Wall Street Journal*, April 19, 2019, https://www.wsj.com/articles/the-answer-to-your-companys-hiring-problem-might-be-right-under-your-nose-11555689542.

48. James Manyika et al., *An Economy that Works: Job Creation and America's Future* (New York: McKinsey Global Institute, 2011), https://www.mckinsey

.com/~/media/McKinsey/Featured%20Insights/Employment%20and %20Growth/An%20economy%20that%20works%20for%20US%20job %20creation/MGI_US_job_creation_full_report.ashx.

49. Frank Greve, "Curb Ramps Liberate Americans with Disabilities—And Everyone Else," McClatchy Newspapers, January 31, 2007, https://www .mcclatchydc.com/news/article24460762.html.

50. U.S. Department of Justice, Civil Rights Division, Public Access Section. The Americans With Disabilities Act: Title II, *Technical Assistance Manual: Covering State and Local Government Programs and Services* (Washington, DC: U.S. Department of Justice, Civil Rights Division, Public Access Section, 2005).

51. Andrea Glover Blackwell, "The Curb-Cut Effect," *Stanford Social Innovation Review* (Winter 2017): 28–33, https://ssir.org/articles/entry/the_curb_cut_ effect#.

52. "Universal Design," Office of Disability Employment Policy, U.S. Department of Labor, accessed August 8, 2020, https://www.dol.gov/agencies/odep/topics/ universal-design.

53. Martin Luther King Jr., "Letter from a Birmingham Jail [King, Jr.]," African Studies Center, University of Pennsylvania, April 16, 1963, https://www.africa .upenn.edu/Articles_Gen/Letter_Birmingham.html.

Chapter 4

1. Colin Magee, Jean Hammond, and Tetyana Astashkina, *The State of Workforce EdTech: A Look at Funding & Innovation in Modern Workforce Education* (Boston: LearnLaunch, 2018), https://learnlaunch.org/wp-content/uploads/ 2018/09/State-of-Workforce_Edtech_LearnLaunch-Sept-2018_-.pdf.

Chapter 5

1. Unless otherwise noted, all interviewee quotes are from Strada Institute for the Future of Work's research titled "Adult Learner Voices," conducted from January 2019 to March 2020.

2. Scott Jaschik and Doug Lederman, "The 2014 Inside Higher Ed Survey of College & University Presidents," Gallup and Inside Higher Ed, 2014, 6, https://www.insidehighered.com/system/files/media/2014PresidentsSurvey-final.pdf.

3. Mark Muro, Robert Maxim, and Jacob Whiton, "Automation and Artificial Intelligence: How Machines Are Affecting People and Places," Brookings,

January 24, 2019, https://www.brookings.edu/research/automation-and-artificial-intelligence-how-machines-affect-people-and-places.

4. Muro, Maxim, and Whiton, "Automation and Artificial Intelligence."

5. Peter Smith, *Free-Range Learning in the Digital Age: The Emerging Revolution in College, Career, and Education* (New York: Select Books, 2018).

6. Although job postings and professional profiles serve as promising data, they are not a perfect data source. Unlike structural labor market data from the Bureau of Labor Statistics and the U.S. Census Bureau, real-time data are not necessarily representative of the entire labor market, though coverage increases each year. Job postings also tend to be skewed by seasonal shifts more than structural labor market data is. Moreover, not all workers have an online professional profile; these workers are not captured in this analysis. Skills listed on professional profiles are not backed by skills assessments, so there is likely great variation in the proficiency of workers who list the same skills, such as project management or knowledge of a particular software package.

At the same time, if nearly all would-be candidates are likely to have a skill, such as the ability to speak English, employers are less likely to list that skill, even though it is a job requirement. Peter Cappelli has also identified what he calls the "Home Depot problem," referring to employers' belief that, for any given job opening, they will find a candidate that is the perfect match—in much the same way that you can be assured of finding the right spare part at Home Depot [Peter Cappelli, *Why Good People Can't Get Jobs: The Skills Gap and What Companies Can Do About It* (Philadelphia: Wharton School Press, 2012)]. Because employers believe the ideal candidate is out there, they often list skills in job postings that are nice to have rather than those that are essential.

Along the same lines, employers tend to advertise less for job openings that are easy to fill because there is already an abundant supply of workers with the skills to fill those jobs. For this reason, postings tend to reflect jobs and roles where there is a gap in the supply and demand for talent in the job market. Finally, traditional labor market information (LMI) has some advantages over skill shapes. Traditional LMI better reflects magnitudes, such as the number of job openings in a given region. Taxonomies are also useful on many occasions, such as when we distinguish between broad knowledge categories, such as mechanical engineering, and discrete skills, such as instrumentation, turbines, product design, or computer-aided design. Taxonomies deal with these conceptual distinctions better than natural-language processing algorithms, which rely on how terms are arranged in sentences. This is why in our research with Emsi, we analyze traditional LMI or structural data alongside job postings and professional profile data.

7. Quoted in Joseph Pistrui, "The Future of Human Work Is Imagination, Creativity, and Strategy," *Harvard Business Review*, January 18, 2018, https://hbr.org/2018/01/the-future-of-human-work-is-imagination-creativity-and-strategy.

8. Chip Cutter, "Amazon to Retrain a Third of Its U.S. Workforce," *The Wall Street Journal*, July 11, 2019. https://www.wsj.com/articles/amazon-to-retrain-a-third-of-its-u-s-workforce-11562841120.

9. Amazon, "Amazon Pledges to Upskill 100,000 U.S. Employees for In-Demand Jobs by 2025," Press release, July 11, 2019, https://press.aboutamazon.com/news-releases/news-release-details/amazon-pledges-upskill-100000-us-employees-demand-jobs-2025.

10. Mike Derezin, "Companies Can Stay Ahead in the Talent War by Recruiting From Within, says this LinkedIn VP," *FastCompany*, June 14, 2019, https://www.fastcompany.com/90363915/companies-can-stay-ahead-in-the-talent-war-by-recruiting-from-within-says-this-linkedin-vp.

11. EMSI SkillsMatch, "Attract and Serve Adult Learners with Personalized Learning Recommendations Powered by Skills," nd, https://www.economicmodeling.com/skills-match/.

12. FutureFit AI, "AI for the Future of Work & Skills," 2020, https://www.futurefit.ai/.

13. SkyHive, "The World's Reskilling Engine," 2020, https://www.skyhive.io/en-ca/enterprise.

14. SkyHive team, interview with author, February 12, 2020.

15. Sean Hinton (CEO of SkyHive), interview with author, January 28, 2020.

16. Sheila Sarem (Founder, Project Basta), interview with Holly Custard, Strada, August 13, 2019.

17. Nitzan Pelman (CEO and Founder, Climb Hire), interview with Holly Custard, Strada, August 21, 2019.

Chapter 6

1. Unless otherwise noted, all interviewee quotes are from Strada Institute for the Future of Work's research titled "Adult Learner Voices," conducted from January 2019 to March 2020

2. Adult learner, interview with Entangled Solutions and Strada Institute for the Future of Work, June–July 2019.

3. Adult learner, interview with Entangled Solutions and Omidyar, September 2018.

4. Alan Berube, "Three Things that Matter for Upward Mobility in the Labor Market," Brookings, January 15, 2019, https://www.brookings.edu/blog/the-avenue/2019/01/15/three-things-that-matter-for-upward-mobility-in-the-labor-market.

5. Adult learner, interview with Entangled Solutions and Strada.

6. Adult learner, interview with Entangled Solutions and Strada.

7. Strada Institute analysis of American Community Survey data, U.S. Census Bureau, 2018: 24 percent of working-class adults don't have health insurance; 31 percent of working-class adults are on food stamps; 16 percent of working-class adults don't have a smartphone; 37 percent of working-class adults don't have a computer; 17 percent of working-class adults don't have internet access; 12 percent of working-class adults don't have access to a vehicle. U.S. Census Bureau, American Community Survey (ACS), One-Year Public Use Microdata Sample (PUMS), 2018, generated by John Ratte using data.census.gov, https://www2.census.gov/programs-surveys/acs/data/pums/2018/1-Year/> accessed via FTP.

8. Quoted in Skip Hollandsworth, "The Power Issue: Michael Sorrell Is Bringing Higher Education to the Students Who Need It Most," *Texas Monthly*, December 2018, https://www.texasmonthly.com/the-culture/power-issue-michael-sorrell-bringing-higher-education-students-need.

9. Michelle Weise, Andrew Hanson, Allison Salisbury, and Kathy Qu, *On-ramps to Good Jobs: Fueling Innovation for the Learning Ecosystem of the Future*, Strada Institute for the Future of Work and Entangled Solutions, January 29, 2019, https://www.stradaeducation.org/report/on-ramps-to-good-jobs/.

10. Adult learner, interview with Entangled Solutions and Strada.

11. Dennis Littky (President, College Unbound; Cofounder, The Met School and Big Picture Learning) and Adam Bush (Cofounder, College Unbound), interview with Holly Custard, Strada, December 4, 2019.

12. Julia Freeland Fisher (Director of Education Research, Clayton Christensen Institute for Disruptive Innovation), interview with Holly Custard, Strada, August 23, 2019.

13. Nitzan Pelman (CEO and Founder, Climb Hire), interview with Holly Custard, Strada, Augst 21, 2019.

14. Pelman interview.

15. Fred Goff (CEO, Jobcase), interview with Jodi Bolognese, Strada, January 15, 2020.

16. Asma Khalid, "This Job Search Website Tries to Be LinkedIn for Everyone Not on LinkedIn," WBUR, January 24, 2018, https://www.wbur.org/bostonomix/2018/01/24/jobcase-online-job-help.

17. Goff interview.

18. Richard Kazis and Freida Molina, "Implementing the WorkAdvance Model: Lessons for Practitioners," Policy Brief, MDRC, October 2016, https://www.mdrc.org/publication/implementing-workadvance-model.

19. Weise et al., *On-ramps to Good Jobs.*

20. Weise et al., *On-ramps to Good Jobs.*

21. Weise et al., *On-ramps to Good Jobs.*

22. Weise et al., *On-ramps to Good Jobs.*

23. Weise et al., *On-ramps to Good Jobs.*

Chapter 7

1. Adult learner, interview with Emsi and Strada Institute for the Future of Work, Summer 2019.

2. Lee Rainie and Janna Anderson, "The Future of Jobs and Jobs Training," Pew Research Center, May 3, 2017, https://www.pewresearch.org/internet/2017/05/03/the-future-of-jobs-and-jobs-training.

3. Unless otherwise noted, all interviewee quotes are from Strada Institute for the Future of Work's research titled "Adult Learner Voices," conducted from January 2019 to March 2020."

4. Strada-Gallup Consumer Insights Survey Data, Strada-Gallup Education Consumer Survey 2016–2019, https://www.stradaeducation.org/network/consumer-insights.

5. Interview with adult learner, Entangled Solutions and Strada Institute for the Future of Work, July 2018. These unpublished interviews were confidential, and the names of interviewees are withheld by mutual agreement.

6. Adult learner, interview with Entangled Solutions and Omidyar.

7. Mark Schneider, "Higher Education Pays: But a Lot More for Some Graduates Than for Others," American Institutes for Research, September 2013, https://www.air.org/sites/default/files/Higher_Education_Pays_Sep_13.pdf.

8. "MIT Graduates Cannot Power a Light Bulb with a Battery," YouTube video, January 21, 2013, 3:08, https://youtu.be/aIhk9eKOLzQ.

9. Michelle Weise, interview with Stephen Kosslyn, "Learning About the Science of Learning: The Minerva Model," Thinking Outside the Sandbox, discontinued podcast audio, May 2017.

10. David J. Epstein, *Range: Why Generalists Triumph in a Specialized World* (New York: Penguin Kindle Edition, 2018).

11. Salman Khan, *The One World Schoolhouse: Education Reimagined* (London: Hodder & Stoughton, 2012).

12. Quoted in Epstein, *Range*.

13. "Productive struggle" is a term in education that describes the process through which learners struggle independently and persevere in problem solving before getting help from a teacher. For more information, please refer to Hiroko Kawaguchi Warshauer, "Productive Struggle in Middle School Mathematics Classrooms," *Journal of Mathematics Teacher Education,* August 14, 2014, https://gato-docs.its.txstate.edu/jcr:fa3bdeec-56a2-43ff-949b-c4d355be763d/10.1007_s10857-014-9286-3.pdf.

14. Science and Technology Policy Office, "Grand Challenges of the 21st Century; Request for Information," Federal Register, February 3, 2010, https://www.federalregister.gov/documents/2010/02/03/2010-2012/grand-challenges-of-the-21st-century-request-for-information.

15. Jason Hyon (Chief Technologist of the Earth Science and Technology Directorate, NASA-Jet Propulsion Laboratory), interview with author, September 2016.

16. Sarah Stein Greenberg, "WIRED By Design: Radical Ideas for Reinventing College, From Stanford's d.School," *WIRED*, November 11, 2014 [video], 18:57, https://www.youtube.com/watch?v=gECAPOpKNyA.

17. Sheryl Estrada, "Millions of US Workers Have 'Limited or No Digital Skills,'" HR Dive, February 11, 2020, https://www.hrdive.com/news/millions-of-us-workers-have-limited-or-no-digital-skills/572048.

18. We also interviewed leaders and the employer partners of other excellent on-ramps such as Urban Alliance, Year Up, and Genesys Works, which are geared more toward younger student populations, as well as Opportunity Youth. There are many similarities in the capabilities and wraparound services

provided in those programs, but we narrowed our focus to on-ramps that are tailored to adults 25 and older.

19. Sandee Kastrul (Cofounder and CEO, i.c.stars), interview with Holly Custard, Strada, June 11, 2019.

20. Ram Katamaraja (CEO, Colaberry), interview with Holly Custard, Strada, February 26, 2019.

21. Katamaraja interview.

22. Rebecca Taber (CEO, Merit America), interview with Holly Custard, Strada, October 31, 2019.

23. Taber interview.

24. Liz Eggleston and Tre Jones, "2014 Programming Bootcamp Survey," Course Report, April 30, 2014, https://www.coursereport.com/2014-programming-bootcamp-survey.pdf.

25. Liz Eggleston, "Coding Bootcamps in 2020, Your Complete Guide to the World of Bootcamps," Course Report, February 11, 2020, https://www.coursereport.com/2020-guide-to-coding-bootcamps-by-course-report.pdf.

26. Ryan Craig, *A New U: Faster + Cheaper Alternatives to College* (Dallas: Ben-Bella Books, 2018).

27. Northeastern University and Gallup, "Facing the Future: U.S., U.K. and Canadian Citizens Call for a Unified Skills Strategy for the AI Age," June 2019, https://www.northeastern.edu/gallup/pdf/Northeastern_Gallup_AI_2019.pdf.

28. Strada Institute for the Future of Work analysis of data from the National Postsecondary Student Aid Survey, 2016. This estimate is based on fall enrollment.

29. The term "skill shape" refers to the unique skill demands associated with a given career field, region, or individual.

Chapter 8

1. Unless otherwise noted, all interviewee quotes are from Strada Institute for the Future of Work's research titled "Adult Learner Voices," conducted from January 2019 to March 2020.

2. Adult learner, interview with Entangled Solutions and Omidyar.

3. Adult learner, interview with Emsi and Strada Institute for the Future of Work.

4. Dan Primack, "Guild Education Raises $157 Million in Series D Funding," Axios, November 13, 2019, https://www.axios.com/guild-education-raises-millions-c6513a48-4480-47d5-a5a3-b82c9ebdf9bc.html.

5. Quoted in Abigail Hess, "Chipotle Is the Latest Company to Spend Millions on This Expensive Benefit for Its Employees—Here's Why," CNBC, October 18, 2019, http://nbr.com/2019/10/18/chipotle-is-the-latest-company-to-spend-millions-on-this-expensive-benefit-for-its-employees-heres-why/.

6. Joseph B. Fuller, Judith K. Wallenstein, Manjari Raman, and Alice de Chalendar, "Future Positive: How Companies Can Tap into Employee Optimism to Navigate Tomorrow's Workplace," BCG Henderson Institute and the Harvard Business School, 2019, https://www.hbs.edu/managing-the-future-of-work/Documents/Future%20Positive%20Report%205.20.pdf, 5.

7. Association for Talent Development, "New Research by ATD: 44 Percent of Organizations Do Not Provide Any Upskilling or Reskilling Opportunities," Press release, June 2018, https://www.td.org/press-release/new-research-by-atd-44-percent-of-organizations-do-not-provide-any-upskilling-or-reskilling-opportunities.

8. Josh Bersin, "Google for Jobs: Potential To Disrupt The $200 Billion Recruiting Industry," Forbes, May 26, 2017, https://www.forbes.com/sites/joshbersin/2017/05/26/google-for-jobs-potential-to-disrupt-the-200-billion-recruiting-industry/#35f930a94d1f.

9. Business Roundtable, "Business Roundtable Redefines the Purpose of a Corporation to Promote 'An Economy That Serves All Americans,'" August 19, 2019, https://www.businessroundtable.org/business-roundtable-redefines-the-purpose-of-a-corporation-to-promote-an-economy-that-serves-all-americans.

10. Anthony Carnevale, Tamara Jayasundera, and Artem Gulish, America's Divided Recovery: College Haves and Have-Nots, (Washington, DC: Georgetown University Center on Education and the Workforce, 2016), https://1gyhoq479ufd3yna29x7ubjn-wpengine.netdna-ssl.com/wp-content/uploads/Americas-Divided-Recovery-web.pdf.

11. Australian Trade and Investment Commission, "Edtech: US Market Snapshot," 2017, https://www.austrade.gov.au/ArticleDocuments/5085/Edtech-US-market-snapshot.pdf.aspx/.

12. Australian Trade and Investment Commission, "Edtech: US Market Snapshot."

13. OECDiLibrary, "Labour Market Programmes: Expenditure and Participants," OECD Employment and Labour Market Statistics, 2015 edition, https://doi.org/10.1787/407f0662-en.

14. Estimated number of program participants who received federal employment and training services = 10,710,359 people. United States Government Accountability Office, Employment and Training Programs, "Department of Labor Should Assess Efforts to Coordinate Services Across Programs," Report to the Permanent Subcommittee on Investigations, Committee on Homeland Security and Governmental Affairs, U.S. Senate, https://www.gao.gov/assets/700/698080.pdf. Total appropriations for training and employment services ($3,428,187,392), Job Corps ($1,702,025,000), employment service/One-Stop ($857,001,539) program administration ($158,656,000) = $6,145,869,931. U. S. Department of Labor Employment and Training Administration, "Summary of Appropriation Budget Authority, Fiscal Year 2017," October 2018, https://www.dol.gov/sites/dolgov/files/ETA/budget/pdfs/17app$_18_1019.pdf.

15. Carnevale et al., *College Is Just the Beginning*.

16. Sandy Baum, Jennifer Ma, Matea Pender, and C. J. Libassi, *Trends in Student Aid 2019*, College Board, November 2019, https://research.collegeboard.org/pdf/trends-student-aid-2019-full-report.pdf.

17. Trace Urdan, "Filling the Other Skills Gap," EdSurge, November 3, 2017, https://www.edsurge.com/news/2017-11-03-filling-the-other-skills-gap.

18. Oren Cass et al., *Works, Skills, Community: Restoring Opportunity for the Working Class*, Opportunity America, Brookings, and the American Enterprise Institute, 2018, http://opportunityamericaonline.org/wp-content/uploads/2018/10/WCG-final_web.pdf.

19. Cass et al., *Works, Skills, Community*.

20. Terah Crewes (Senior Partner, Entangled Solutions), interview with author, November 1, 2019.

21. All details regarding Walmart in this section of the chapter come from Harvard Taskforce on Skills and Employability, "Walmart Site Visit Notes," November 1, 2019, in author's possession. Used with permission.

22. Sallyann Della Casa (CEO, GLEAC), interview with Holly Custard, Strada, February 10, 2020.

23. FRED, Federal Reserve Bank of St. Louis, Board of Governors of the Federal Reserve System (US), "Student Loans Owned and Securitized, Outstanding (SLOAS)," https://fred.stlouisfed.org/series/SLOAS.

24. Tonio Sorrento (CEO, Vemo Education), interview with Holly Custard, Strada, July 26, 2019.

25. AZF Scrapbook, "Life Capital Conference," March 30, 2019, https://azfuller.com/2019/03/30/life-capital-conference.

26. Andrew P. Kelly and Kevin James, "Untapped Potential: Making the Higher Education Market Work for Students and Taxpayers," AEI Series on Reforming Quality Assurance in Higher Education, Center on Higher Education Reform, October 2014, https://www.aei.org/wp-content/uploads/2014/10/Untapped-Potential-corr.pdf.

27. Sorrento interview.

28. Nitzan Pelman (CEO, Climb Hire), interview with Holly Custard, Strada, August 21, 2019.

29. Sandee Kastrul (Cofounder and CEO, i.c.stars), interview with Holly Custard, Strada, June 11, 2019.

30. Tracy Palandjian (CEO and cofounder of Social Finance), interview with author, February 26, 2020, https://stradaeducation.zoom.us/rec/share/y8ZJc42o5zhJYq_j6k6HAKo-Qpbfeaa81CJL8vUNyE83ezOKZnieEOVdTWLfl08G.

31. Lauren Weber, "A Counterintuitive Fix for Robot-driven Unemployment," *The Wall Street Journal*, January 6, 2020, https://www.wsj.com/articles/a-counterintuitive-fix-for-robot-driven-unemployment-11578331272?mod=searchresults&page=1&pos=2.

32. Including Senators Cantwell (D-WA) and Snowe (R-ME), and Reps. Emanuel (D-IL), Ramstad (R-MN), Larson (D-CT), Polis (D-CO), Kilmer (D-WA), Roskam (R-IL), and Paulsen (R-MN).

33. Alastair Fitzpayne and Ethan Pollack, "Lifelong Learning and Training Accounts: Helping Workers Adapt and Succeed in a Changing Economy," Aspen Institute Future of Work Initiative Issue Brief, May 24, 2018, https://www.aspeninstitute.org/publications/lifelong-learning-and-training-accounts-2018/.

34. Fitzpayne and Pollack, "Lifelong Learning," 1.

Chapter 9

1. Quoted in Jonathan Vanian, "Why Corporate Recruiters Should Not Be So Obsessed with Prestigious College Degrees," *Fortune*, June 26, 2018, https://fortune.com/2018/06/26/fortune-ceo-initiative-workforce-skills.

2. "Ladders, Inc. Expands Resume Reviewer and Unveils Trends in Resume Errors," Ladders, December 8, 2016, https://www.theladders.com/press/ladders-inc-expands-resume-reviewer-unveils-trends-resume-errors.

3. Jeff Cox, "It's Never Been This Hard for Companies to Find Qualified Workers," CNBC, February 19, 2020, https://www.cnbc.com/2020/02/19/its-never-been-this-hard-for-companies-to-find-qualified-workers.html.

4. U. S. Chamber of Commerce Foundation, "Hiring in the Modern Talent Marketplace," February 4, 2020, https://www.uschamberfoundation.org/sites/default/files/2020_USCCF_ModernTalentMarketplaceHiring.pdf.

5. Joseph B. Fuller and Manjari Raman, "Dismissed by Degrees: How Degree Inflation is Undermining US Competitiveness and Hurting America's Middle Class" (Cambridge, MA: Accenture, Grads of Life, and Harvard Business School, 2017), https://www.hbs.edu/managing-the-future-of-work/Documents/dismissed-by-degrees.pdf.

6. Fuller and Raman, "Dismissed by Degrees."

7. Peter Cappelli, "Your Approach to Hiring Is All Wrong," *Harvard Business Review*, June 2019, https://hbr.org/2019/05/recruiting.

8. Ryan Craig, "Will Employment Law Help Break the Higher Education Monopoly?" *Real Clear Education*, June 16, 2017, https://www.realcleareducation.com/articles/2017/06/16/will_employment_law_help_break_the_higher_education_monopoly_110167.html.

9. Peter Q. Blair et al., "Searching for STARs: Work Experience as a Job Market Signal for Workers without Bachelor's Degrees," National Bureau of Economic Research Working Paper no. 26844, March 2020, https://www.nber.org/papers/w26844.

10. Corinne Moss-Racusin et al., "Science Faculty's Subtle Gender Biases Favor Male Students," *PNAS* 109, no. 41 (October 9, 2012): 16474–16479, https://doi.org/10.1073/pnas.1211286109.

11. Riia O'Donnell, "Skills-Based Hiring Will Shift the Marketplace, Experts Say," HR Dive, October 12, 2017, https://www.hrdive.com/news/skills-based-hiring-will-shift-the-marketplace-experts-say/506970.

12. U.S. Chamber of Commerce Foundation, "Hiring in the Modern Talent Marketplace."

13. LinkedIn Corporate Communications, "New LinkedIn Research Explores the Shift Toward Skills-Based Hiring," September 16, 2019, https://news.linkedin.com/2019/January/new-linkedin-research-xxplores-the-shift-toward-skills-based-hir.

14. CFA Staff, "The Coming Paradigm Shift in Competency-Based Hiring: An Interview with Innovate+Educate," Southern New Hampshire University, College for America, April 12, 2017, https://collegeforamerica.org/competency-based-hiring.

15. Quoted in Andrew Kreighbaum, "Business Group Backs Expanding Access to Aid," *Inside Higher Ed*, June 13, 2019, https://www.insidehighered.com/quicktakes/2019/06/13/business-group-backs-expanding-access-aid.

16. Glassdoor Team, "15 More Companies That No Longer Require a Degree—Apply Now," Glassdoor, January 10, 2020, https://www.glassdoor.com/blog/no-degree-required/.

17. Wiley Education Services & Future Workplace, "Closing the Skills Gap 2019" Wiley edu, LLC, September 2019, https://edservices.wiley.com/wp-content/uploads/2019/08/201908-CSG-Report-WES-FINAL.pdf.

18. Sean R. Gallagher, "Educational Credentials Come of Age: A Survey on the Use and Value of Educational Credentials in Hiring," Northeastern University Center for the Future of Higher Education and Talent Strategy, December 2018, https://www.northeastern.edu/cfhets/wp-content/uploads/2018/12/Educational_Credentials_Come_of_Age_2018.pdf.

19. Credential Engine, "Counting U.S. Postsecondary and Secondary Credentials," September 2019, https://credentialengine.org/counting-credentials-2019-report/.

20. Alfred N. Whitehead, *The Aims of Education and Other Essays* (New York: The Free Press, 1929), 32.

21. Quoted in Greg Whiteley, dir., *Most Likely to Succeed* [documentary] (2015; Boston, MA: EDU21C Foundation, 2018).

22. Meagan Wilson, Martin Kurzweil, and Rayane Alamuddin, *Mapping the Wild West of Pre-Hire Assessment: A Landscape View of the Uncharted Technology-Facilitated Ecosystem* (New York: Ithaka S+R, 2018), https://sr.ithaka.org/publications/mapping-the-wild-west-of-pre-hire-assessment.

23. David J. Epstein, *Range: Why Generalists Triumph in a Specialized World* (New York: Penguin Kindle Edition, 2018), 11.

24. Tracy M. Kantrowitz, Kathy Tuzinski, and Justin Raines, "2018 Global Assessment Trends Report," SHL, 2018, https://www.shl.com/en/assessments/trends/global-assessment-trends-report.

25. Claudia Goldin and Cecilia Rouse, "Orchestrating Impartiality: The Impact of 'Blind' Auditions on Female Musicians," National Bureau of Economic

Research Working Paper no. 5903, January 1997, https://www.nber.org/papers/w5903.

26. Richard Shavelson, "The Spellings Commission Report and the Collegiate Learning Assessment," Forum for the Future of Higher Education, 2008, http://forum.mit.edu/articles/the-spellings-commission-report-and-the-collegiate-learning-assessment.

27. Shavelson, "Spellings Commission Report."

28. Rebecca Kantar (CEO, Imbellus), interview with author, November 11, 2019.

29. Upfront Ventures, "Rebecca Kantar Presents Imbellus | Upfront Summit 2017," YouTube video, 9:56, March 2, 2017, https://www.youtube.com/watch?v=r4zVktAXafE.

30. Ananth Kasturiraman and Caroline Fay (Cofounders, Skillist), interview with Holly Custard, Strada, January 28, 2019.

31. Parker Dewey, "How Career Launcher Payments Work," https://info.parkerdewey.com/how-career-launcher-payments-work.

32. Skillful, "How Skills-Based Hiring Practices Can Help You Find the Talent You Need," February 7, 2019, https://www.skillful.com/skills-based-hiring-practices.

33. Adele Peters, "The Body Shop Will Start Hiring the First Person Who Applies for Any Retail Job," FastCompany, February 12, 2020, https://www.fastcompany.com/90462746/the-body-shop-will-start-hiring-the-first-person-who-applies-for-any-retail-job.

34. Lindsay Northon et al., "2016 Human Capital Benchmarking Report," SHRM, November 2016, https://www.shrm.org/hr-today/trends-and-forecasting/research-and-surveys/pages/2016-human-capital-report.aspx.

35. Heather Terenzio (CEO, Techtonic), interview with Holly Custard, Strada, January 29, 2019.

36. Ryan Craig, "Employers Seeking to 'Try Before They Buy' Will Change Career Paths for College Grads," Forbes, 2018, https://www.forbes.com/sites/ryancraig/2018/09/06/employers-seeking-to-try-before-they-buy-will-change-career-paths-for-college-grads/#60c52c082834.

37. Terenzio interview.

38. Michelle Weise, Andrew Hanson, Allison Salisbury, and Kathy Qu, On-ramps to Good Jobs: Fueling Innovation for the Learning Ecosystem of the Future, Strada Institute for the Future of Work and Entangled Solutions, January 29, 2019, https://www.stradaeducation.org/report/on-ramps-to-good-jobs/.

39. Chok Ooi (Cofounder and CEO) and Emily Wattman-Turner (VP of Operations), interview with author, May 17, 2018.

40. Registered apprenticeships are those registered with and approved by the Department of Labor based on its quality standards. Elka Torpey and Ryan Farrell, "Apprenticeships: Outlook and Wages in Selected Occupations," November 2019, https://www.bls.gov/careeroutlook/2019/article/apprenticeships-outlook-wages-update.htm

41. Alex Bell et al., "Who Becomes an Inventor in America? The Importance of Exposure to Innovation," *The Quarterly Journal of Economics* 134, no. 2 (November 29, 2018): 647–713, https://doi.org/10.1093/qje/qjy028.

42. Catherine Ashcraft and Anthony Breitzman, *Who Invents It? Women's Participation in Information Technology Patenting, 2012 Update* (Boulder, CO: National Center for Women & Information Technology, 2012), https://www.ncwit.org/sites/default/files/resources/2012whoinventsit_web_1.pdf.

43. Michelle R. Weise and Janet Salm, "On-Ramps to Good Jobs: The Benefits for Employers," Solutions from Beyond the Beltway, Manhattan Institute, December 19, 2019, https://www.manhattan-institute.org/employee-training-on-ramp.

Chapter 10

1. Paul Rogers and Darren McAvoy, "Mule Deer Impede Pando's Recovery: Implications for Aspen Resilience From a Single-Genotype Forest," *PLoS ONE* 13, no. 10 (October 17, 2018), https://doi.org/10.1371/journal.pone.0203619.

2. JoAnna Klein, "Pando, the Most Massive Organism on Earth, Is Shrinking," *The New York Times*, October 17, 2018, https://www.nytimes.com/2018/10/17/science/pando-aspens-utah.html.

3. Suzanne Simard, "How Trees Talk to Each Other," TEDSummit, video, 18:11, June 2016, https://www.ted.com/talks/suzanne_simard_how_trees_talk_to_each_other/transcript.

4. Steven A. Cohen and Matthew W. Granade, "Models Will Run the World," *The Wall Street Journal*, August 19, 2018, https://www.wsj.com/articles/models-will-run-the-world-1534716720.

5. Anthony P. Carnevale, "Comment on the Notice of Proposed Rulemaking Regarding Gainful Employment," Georgetown Center on Education and the Workforce, Policy, Public Comments, August 17, 2010, https://cew.georgetown.edu/policy/.

6. Matt Gee (Cofounder and CEO, BrightHive), interview with Holly Custard, Strada, March 19, 2019.

7. Gee interview.

8. Gee interview.

Conclusion

1. Edward Alden and Laura Taylor-Kale, *The Work Ahead: Machines, Skills, and US Leadership in the Twenty-First Century*, The Council on Foreign Relations, Independent Task Force Report no. 76, April 2018, https://www.cfr.org/report/the-work-ahead/report.

2. Daron Acemoglu and Pascual Restrepo, "Artificial Intelligence, Automation and Work," NBER Working Paper No. 24196, January 2018, https://www.nber.org/papers/w24196.

3. Nick Wingfield, "As Amazon Pushes Forward with Robots, Workers Find New Roles," *The New York Times*, September 10, 2017, https://www.nytimes.com/2017/09/10/technology/amazon-robots-workers.html.

4. David Autor, "Polanyi's Paradox and the Shape of Employment Growth," NBER Working Paper no. 20485, September 2014, doi:10.3386/w20485.

5. John Oliver, "Warehouses: Last Week Tonight with John Oliver (HBO)," YouTube video, 21:17, July 1, 2019, https://www.youtube.com/watch?v=d9m7d07k22A.

6. Jessica Silver-Greenberg and Natalie Kitroeff, "Miscarrying at Work: The Physical Toll of Pregnancy Discrimination," *The New York Times*, October 21, 2018, https://www.nytimes.com/interactive/2018/10/21/business/pregnancy-discrimination-miscarriages.html.

7. Silver-Greenberg and Kitroeff, "Miscarrying at Work."

8. Mary Gray and Siddharth Suri, *Ghost Work: How to Stop Silicon Valley from Building a New Global Underclass* (Boston: Houghton Mifflin Harcourt, 2019), 10.

9. Gray and Suri, *Ghost Work*, xvii.

10. Rob Nail, "Introduction to Singularity University" (site visit, Singularity University, Santa Clara, CA, June 8, 2017).

11. Brian David Johnson, "Foreword: How to Invent the Future," *Trend Magazine* (Spring 2017), https://www.pewtrusts.org/en/trend/archive/summer-2017/foreword-how-to-invent-the-future.

ACKNOWLEDGMENTS

The great American poet Emily Dickinson once lamented out of exasperation to her friend Samuel Bowles, the editor of Springfield's *The Republican*: "The old words are numb—and there a'nt any new ones." Out of her disappointment with language, she created an entirely new kind of diction by stopping and starting our words and breath with startling and frequent dashes. She bent language toward newness—always relying, however, on the existing old one.

Out of the old comes the new. A new innovation is rarely born from nothing. It is often a work of palimpsest. "Palimpsest" is the word for a manuscript that has been scraped and rubbed smooth and then written upon again. In the act of erasure, you cannot help but leave traces of the text before. This intriguing word captures the way in which there is really no such thing as an original work. Everything we do connects to something before. Painters do this all the time—paint over old paintings on the same canvas. We build and build toward something we hope is new, but all of that supposed newness is inevitably connected to the old or someone before.

In a book like this, the hope is to create newness from the borrowed greatness of others. So much smart work has been put forward by many thinkers, economists, philosophers, futurists, neuroscientists, data analysts, and educators. Some of these great findings, however, are locked behind paywalls, siloed in academic journals, tucked away in niche blog posts, or discussed at conferences that most people don't attend. I hope this book serves as a harvesting of sorts of some of the incredible richness of data and insights out there already.

To my mentors, Clayton Christensen and Michael Horn, thank you for all you've taught me.

To my brilliant team at Strada Institute for the Future of Work, I am so grateful to have worked with you: Janet Salm, Holly Custard, Emily Cole, Melissa Leavitt, and our alumni and partners, including Beth Bean, Andrew Hanson, Yustina Saleh, Rob Sentz, Lora Louise Broady, Rob Kadel, Linzy Farmerie, Jodi Bolognese, Kat Jiang, Erica Kim, Monica Herk, and Tiffane Cochran. You have all helped make this book possible.

At the same time, none of this would have been possible without our interviewees who shared their stories with us. We thank you sincerely for your vulnerability, and we're so glad to have met you through our friends at Omidyar, College Unbound, i.c.stars, PelotonU, SV Academy, Conexus Indiana, Climb Hire, Merit America, JVS, STRIVE, Entangled Solutions, and Refactored.ai. We're especially indebted to Dennis Littky and Adam Bush at College Unbound for helping us jump-start this work by connecting us with their amazing students and staff. Holly, the interviews you facilitated and videos you produced with Aled Ordu were the secret sauce and starting point for so much of the qualitative research.

I would be remiss if I didn't thank the entire team and board at Strada Education Network, and especially Strada Institute's advisory committee members for their enthusiastic support of our work: Alex Alonso, Sandy Baum, James Canton, Anthony Carnevale, Ryan Craig, Joseph Fuller, Mary Gray, Earl Lewis, Stephen Moret, Joel Meyerson, Cheryl Oldham, Jeff Selingo, Peter Smith, Mimi Strouse, Johnny Taylor, Van Ton-Quinlivan, Deb Quazzo, and Craig Weidemann.

In addition, I want to thank Gunnar Counselman, Ellie Pojarska, Brian Fleming, Wil Zemp, Sally Johnstone, Kate Kinast, Victor Cortez, Elizabeth Redcay, Joanna Swerdlow, Michelle Dervan,

Dre Bennin, Ben Wildavsky, the neighborhood crew in Johnson Acres, the team at Imaginable Futures, Wiley, as well as the entire Stern Strategy team.

Finally, to the most important people in my life: my husband, Mike, and my children, Noe and Logan. We did it, Team Weise! Thank you, love, for all of the weekends when you whisked the kids away to give me time to write this book. To my parents, who sacrificed so much for me and my brother, David: We are both forever grateful. And because there are too many of you to name, thank you to my entire family and my dear friends for your unconditional love.

ABOUT THE AUTHOR

Michelle R. Weise, Ph.D., is an entrepreneur-in-residence and senior advisor at Imaginable Futures, a venture of The Omidyar Group. Michelle's work over the last decade has concentrated on preparing working-age adults for the jobs of today and tomorrow. She was the chief innovation officer of Strada Education Network's Institute for the Future of Work and Sandbox Collaborative, the innovation center of Southern New Hampshire University. With Clayton Christensen, she coauthored *Hire Education: Mastery, Modularization, and the Workforce Revolution* (2014) while leading the higher education practice at the Clayton Christensen Institute for Disruptive Innovation. Her commentaries on redesigning higher education and developing more innovative workforce and talent pipeline strategies have been featured in *The Economist, The Wall Street Journal, The New York Times*, and *Harvard Business Review* and on *PBS Newshour*.

She has also served on Massachusetts Governor Baker's Commission on Digital Innovation and Lifelong Learning, the American Academy of Arts and Sciences' Commission on the Future of Undergraduate Education, and the Harvard Skills and Employability Task Force. Michelle is a former Fulbright Scholar and graduate of Harvard and Stanford. She lives with her family in the North Shore of Massachusetts.

INDEX

Page references followed by *fig* indicate an illustrated figure.

F

Facebook, 12, 131
Facial expressions, 10
Family Resource Center (Los Angeles Valley College), 98
Far transfer, 117
Federal financial aid system, 34, 146–147
50+ workers, 52–55
"Filter bubbles," 10
Finland's "1 percent AI initiative," 12, 13
Fisher, Julia Freeland, 103
Fishlake National Forest (Utah), 181–182
Flatiron School, 131
Flow, 173
Flynn, James, 118
Food stamps, 97
For-profit colleges
  federal financial aid system and, 34
  flexible learning experiences, 115
  predatory practices, 32
  quality issues, 33*fig*–34
  UP Fund, 158
  value proposition and consumption amenities of, 34–36*fig*
  work-life balance, 115
  See also Higher education institutions
Freshman Survey, 18
Frye, Marilyn, 56
Fuller, Joseph, 51, 144
Funding/financial issues
  federal financial aid system and student debt, 23, 34, 146–147
  having enough funding to pursue education, 139–144
  innovative approaches to funding, 148–158
  philanthropic funding resources, 147–148

Steve's story on accessing information on funding, 69–70
  venture capital funding, 147
Funding models
  career impact bonds, 155
  Future of Work Initiative (Aspen Institute), 157–158
  income share agreements (ISAs), 151–155
  Lifelong Learning Accounts (LiLAs), 156–158
  outskilling, 155–156
  SkillsFuture (Singapore), 156–157
  FutureFit, 88, 155–156
  Future of Work Initiative (Aspen Institute), 157–158
The Fuzzy and the Techie (Hartley), 11

G

Gallagher, Sean, 45
Gallup–Northeastern survey, 46
Garbage in, garbage out problem, 188
Gee, Matt, 185–187, 188
Gender differences, underemployment and, 21
Gene editing, 194
General Assembly, 131
"Genius of the AND," 11
Gentner, Dedre, 118–119
Gen Z "birth dearth," 24
Georgia Department of Economic Development, 184
Ghost Work (Gray and Suri), 193
Gibson, William, 58
Gig work
  part-time employment including, 70
  virtual communities for networking, 106
Gilbert, Clark, 44
GitHub, 171*fig*–173
GlassDoor, 105, 159

On-ramps
  targeted education opportunities of,
    125–126, 133
On-the-job training, 50, 126
Open hiring, 173–174
Open loop university concept, 15
Opioid abuse, 60
Opportunity@Work, 161, 170
Opportunity gap, 58–60
Outskilling, 155–156
Outsourced apprenticeship model,
  174–177

P

Pachovas, Michael, 63
Palandjian, Tracy, 155
Pando (aspen trees root system),
  181–182
Pariser, Eli, 10
Parker Dewey, 170
Part-time employment
  Steve's story on funding education
    through, 70
  working class adults engaged in,
    62–63
Paul Quinn College (South Dallas,
  Texas), 98–99
Pelman, Nitzan, 89–90, 103–104, 105,
  154
People with disabilities, 63
Performance
  disruptive innovation for, 26–27
  first iterations of innovations for
    improved, 28*fig*–29
  sustaining innovation for, 29*fig*–30,
    31–32
Per Scholas, 178
Personal computers (PCs), 30–31, 32,
  38
Personalized learning, 114–115
Pew Research Center
  on baby boomer population, 52

on workers' self-reporting need for
  training, 45
Philadelphia Works, 107
Philanthropic funding resources,
  147–148
Polanyi's paradox, 7
Pluralsight, 70
Polanyi, Michael, 7
PolicyLink, 63
Populations of users, 27*fig*–28
Postsecondary education
  academic silos within, 117–118
  applying closed-loop concept to, 183
  community college statistics on, 46
  connecting to K–12 education,
    workforce development,
    183–185
  creating value network of employers,
    47
  failure to accommodate working
    learners, 112–114
  funding stream for $655 billion
    industry of, 48
  jobs of the future will require more,
    61–63
  MOOCs option for, 41, 45, 70
  need for and directions of innovation
    in, 26–27, 32–43, 48
  the new consumers of, 45–46
  recasting as an ecosystem, 57–58
  Steve's story on his need for, 67–71
  See also Higher education; Workforce
    training
Postsecondary education innovation
  autonomous growth units, 39–40
  CBE potential for disruptive, 41–43
  enormous room for, 48
  integrated learning ecosystem,
    148–158
  modularized learning, 42–43
  navigable learning ecosystem, 82–90
  need for disruptive innovation,
    26–27, 32–38

Technical skills (*continued*)
needed for job transition, 83–88
need for hybrid human and, 11–12
need ways to translate from one
industry to another, 81–82
postsecondary education driven by
need for, 45–46
a skills compass to identify worker,
86–88
tech-enabled skills acquisition of, 129
T-shaped learner combining
knowledge and, 14*fig*
See also Human + technical skills
Technological advancements
able to be utilized by users, 29*fig*–30
automation, 7, 8–9*fig*, 59, 191–192
changing people as well as nature of
work, 10
LinkedIn's top jobs (2014) created
through, 5
new skills and knowledge required
by, 4
possible destructive networking
effects of, 11–12
preparing for future trends of, 7
shaping our social relationships and
perceptions, 10–11
See also Artificial intelligence (AI)
Techtonic, 175
Tencent, 182
Terenzio, Heather, 175–176
360-degree support services, 97, 102
Time and financial barriers
innovative approaches to overcome
funding and, 148–158
to workers seeking additional
education or training, 139–144
Toyota, 31, 32, 188
Trader Joe's, 90
Transfer of learning, 117
Transparency
AI and issue of, 13
data trusts, 186, 187–188

of educational options for working
learners, 79
a healthy future learning ecosystem
will enable, 195
income sharing agreements (ISAs),
152–153
lacking on philanthropic investments,
147
Transparent learning ecosystem
credential-based hiring, 161–164
introduction to concept of, 73
learning benefits of a, 159
limited visibility into hiring process
predicament, 160–161
moving toward skills-based hiring,
161–164
problem of hiring process frustration,
159–160
seeds of innovation toward
skills-based hiring, 165–179
Transparent skills-based hiring
innovation
blind and performance-based
internships, 170
blind audition concept, 165–166
Collegiate Learning Assessment
(CLA), 166–167
GitHub, 171*fig*–173
leveraging blind assessment tools,
173–174
open hiring, 173–174
scenario-based assessment, 167–169
Skillist matchmaking tool, 169–170
SkillMetric exam, 167
"try before you buy" outsourced
apprenticeships, 174–177
Transportation access
providing MetroCards for, 98, 100
wraparound supports to help with,
94–95
Tree root systems, 181–182
"Try before you buy" outsourced
apprenticeships, 174–177

T-shape learner, 14*fig*
"Tyranny of the OR," 11

U

UberEats program, 106
Uber Houston, 106
Udemy, 70
Underemployment phenomenon,
20–21
Unemployed
working class adults among the,
59–60
Work, Skills, Community report on,
59
United States
challenge of opportunity gap in the,
58–60
challenges of aging population in the,
53
declining life expectancy in the, 60
impact of COVID-19 pandemic on
workers in the, 19, 50–51
low OECD ranking on investing
taxpayer-funded training of the,
146
sole hiring use of competency-based
assessments prohibited in the,
55
University of California–San Francisco
(UCSF), 126
University of Chicago, 185
University of Michigan, 36
University of Otago (New Zealand),
118
University of Phoenix, 32, 33, 35
University of Texas, 35–36
University Ventures, 152
Upcredentialing (or credential
inflation), 161
UP Fund, 155
UPS, 124
US Department of Education, 183
US Department of Labor, 175

Users
circle diagram representing
populations of, 27*fig*–28
improvements that can be absorbed
by, 29*fig*–30
nonconsumers, 27, 30–31
sustaining innovations that can be
used by, 29*fig*–30
U.S. News & World Report, 80, 183
UT-Southwestern, 99

V

Value proposition, description of, 36*fig*
Van Kleunen, Andy, 61
Vemo Education, 152
Venture capital funding, 147
Virginia government agencies' data
trust, 188
Virtual and augmented reality, 123–125
Virtual communities
building social capital through, 105
Jobcase, 105–106
Virtual reality (AR), 123–125
The Voice (TV show), 165–166

W

Wall Street Journal, 156
Walmart, 148–149, 184
Walmart Academies, 148–149
Washington, DC skill shape, 136*fig*
The Water of Systems Change (Kania), 57
Weber, Lauren, 156
Weise, Michelle, 36, 41, 136, 137
Western Governors University (WGU),
35, 40
Western Interstate Commission for
Higher Education, 23–24
Wharton School (University of
Pennsylvania), 49, 161
Whitehead, Alfred North, 164
White House National Economic
Council, 58